MW00423978

There are several good books on how to prepare and deliver sermons, but there are other pressing questions that we must answer. Why do expositional preaching? Why regard preaching the Word as the center of the church's worship, edification, and evangelism? How can we listen to expositional preaching to benefit the most from it? David Strain responds to these questions (and more) with brief, biblical, and heartwarming answers. This is an excellent book for pastors, seminary students, and the people who hear them preach.

—**Joel R. Beeke**, President, Puritan Reformed Theological Seminary

David Strain has given us his against-the-stream argument for expositional preaching. He's heard all the gripes and objections to it (and deftly handles them in his own Q&A). His case is evenly balanced yet with an edge that cuts in all the right places. Is it too much to hope that elders and deacons will digest it—as well as all personal-devotion, small-group, online-preaching addicts? How refreshing to read a work that agrees with the orneriness of God in insisting on the supremacy of preaching in the local church.

—**Dale Ralph Davis**, Minister in Residence, First Presbyterian Church, Columbia, South Carolina

In a day and age when the Word of God must compete with so many things that distract and vie for our hearts, David Strain opens the pages of the Bible to show the church why hearing the Bible preached is so vital to the Christian life. If you struggle to benefit from preaching, then this little book is the perfect tonic to invigorate your appreciation for the Word of God. Pick it up to see why "the foolishness of preaching" contains Christ's words of wisdom, grace, and eternal life.

—**J. V. Fesko**, Harriett Barbour Professor of Systematic and Historical Theology, Reformed Theological Seminary, Jackson

David Strain has given us a thoughtful, engaging, stimulating primer on the importance of hearing God's Word. As a seasoned pastor, Strain understands how vital it is for church members to hear God's Word rightly and have it shape how they think and live. In these rapidly changing and unsettling times, I am convinced that the health of the church depends on its taking to heart the principles and convictions Strain so plainly and passionately sets out in this little gem. A must-read for church members and pastors alike.

—**Ian Hamilton**, Professor of Systematic and Historical Theology, Greenville Presbyterian Theological Seminary

Undoubtedly, books written with "wisdom from above" on preaching are a blessing. Now David Strain, in God's providence, has given us a book written with "wisdom from above" on hearing the Word preached. This book is biblical, readable, and engaging. *Tolle lege!*

—**Harry L. Reeder III**, Senior Pastor, Briarwood Presbyterian Church, Birmingham

EXPOSITORY
PREACHING

BLESSINGS OF THE FAITH
A Series

Jason Helopoulos
Series Editor

Covenantal Baptism, by Jason Helopoulos
Expository Preaching, by David Strain
Persistent Prayer, by Guy M. Richard

EXPOSITORY
PREACHING

DAVID STRAIN

PUBLISHING
P.O. BOX 817 • PHILLIPSBURG • NEW JERSEY 08865-0817

If you find this book helpful, consider writing a review online
—or contact P&R at editorial@prpbooks.com with your comments.
We'd love to hear from you.

© 2021 by David Strain

All rights reserved. No part of this book may be reproduced, stored in a retrieval system, or transmitted in any form or by any means—electronic, mechanical, photocopy, recording, or otherwise—except for brief quotations for the purpose of review or comment, without the prior permission of the publisher, P&R Publishing Company, P.O. Box 817, Phillipsburg, New Jersey 08865-0817.

Scripture quotations are from the ESV® Bible (The Holy Bible, English Standard Version®), copyright © 2001 by Crossway, a publishing ministry of Good News Publishers. Used by permission. All rights reserved.

Italics within Scripture quotations indicate emphasis added.

Printed in the United States of America

Library of Congress Cataloging-in-Publication Data

Names: Strain, David, author.
Title: Expository preaching / David Strain.
Description: Phillipsburg, New Jersey : P&R Publishing, [2021] | Series:
  Blessings of the faith | Summary: "Informative, encouraging, and
  practical, this short book serves as a helpful primer on expositional
  preaching and its place in the life of a Christian and the worship of
  the church"-- Provided by publisher.
Identifiers: LCCN 2021015015 | ISBN 9781629958507 (hardcover) | ISBN
  9781629958514 (epub) | ISBN 9781629958521 (mobi)
Subjects: LCSH: Expository preaching.
Classification: LCC BV4211.3 .S77 2021 | DDC 251--dc23
LC record available at https://lccn.loc.gov/2021015015

For my wife, Sheena, who never fails to encourage me even when submerged beneath great trials of her own.

CONTENTS

FOREWORD

It has often been said—sometimes with a sense of humor and sometimes in annoyance—that Presbyterian and Reformed churches love to do things "decently and in order." I can understand both the humor and the frustration that lie behind that sentiment. We love our plans, our minutes, our courts, and our committees. Presbyterian and Reformed folks have been known to appoint committees just to oversee other committees (reminding me of the old *Onion* headline that announced "New Starbucks Opens in Rest Room of Existing Starbucks"). We like doing things so decently that we expect our church officers to know three things: the Bible, our confessions, and a book with *Order* in its title.

But before we shake our heads in disbelief at those uber-Reformed types (physician, heal thyself!), we should recall that before "decently and in order" was a Presbyterian predilection, it was a biblical command (see 1 Cor. 14:40). Paul's injunction for the church to be marked by propriety and decorum, to be well-ordered like troops drawn up in ranks, is a fitting conclusion to a portion of Scripture that deals with confusion regarding gender, confusion at the Lord's Table, confusion about spiritual gifts, confusion in the body of Christ, and confusion in public worship. "Decently and in order" sounds pretty good compared to the mess that prevailed in Corinth.

A typical knock on Presbyterian and Reformed Christians is that though supreme in head, they are deficient in heart. We are the emotionless stoics, the changeless wonders, God's frozen chosen. But such veiled insults would not have impressed the apostle Paul, for he knew that the opposite of order in the church is not free-flowing spontaneity; it is self-exalting chaos. God never favors confusion over peace (see 1 Cor. 14:33). He never pits theology against doxology or head against heart. David Garland put it memorably, "The Spirit of ardor is also the Spirit of order."[1]

When Jason Helopoulos approached me about writing a foreword for this series, I was happy to oblige—not only because Jason is one of my best friends (and we both root for the hapless Chicago Bears) but because these careful, balanced, and well-reasoned volumes will occupy an important place on the book stalls of Presbyterian and Reformed churches. We need short, accessible books written by thoughtful, seasoned pastors for regular members on the foundational elements of church life and ministry. That's what we need, and that's what this series delivers: wise answers to many of the church's most practical and pressing questions.

This series of books on Presbyterian and Reformed theology, worship, and polity is not a multivolume exploration of 1 Corinthians 14:40, but I am glad it is unapologetically written with Paul's command in mind. The reality is that every church will worship in some way, pray in some way, be led in some way, be structured in some way, and do baptism and the Lord's Supper in some way. Every church is living out some form of theology—even if that theology is based on pragmatism instead of biblical principles. Why wouldn't we want the life we share in the church to be shaped by the best exegetical, theological, and historical reflections? Why wouldn't we want to be thoughtful instead of thoughtless? Why wouldn't we want all things in the life we live together to be done decently and in good order? That's not the Presbyterian and Reformed way. That's God's way, and Presbyterian and Reformed Christians would do well not to forget it.

Kevin DeYoung
Senior Pastor, Christ Covenant Church
Matthews, North Carolina

Introduction

WHAT DO YOU SAY TO STEVE AND RACHEL?

Steve and his wife Rachel have been visiting your church for about six months. You've gotten to know them both a little, and, as part of the "greeters ministry" at your church, you've come to visit them in their home and welcome them to the fellowship. You ask about their story and what brought them to the congregation.

"Well, the truth is we've been sort of drifting for a while," Steve replies. "My wife and I were both raised in small country Baptist congregations, and that's where we came to know the Lord. They loved us well and discipled us faithfully. After college we started attending a local Bible church with friends, and the welcome we received and the practical messages we heard from the front really made a difference in our lives."

"But then our daughter, who was a senior in college at the time, was hit by a drunk driver late one night," Rachel says. "Our lives changed forever. We buried her two years ago, and that's when we began looking for something different in church. I guess the short, upbeat messages that were so much a part of the Sunday worship experience in our church started to sound hollow. Bouncing along with happy music and listening to teaching that skimmed across the surface of both the Bible and the hard realities of our lives at that time left us dissatisfied. We needed something more."

Steve picks up the story. "We tried various options. We've even stayed home and tried listening to preachers online. But none of that really worked out. And then, about six months ago, a friend invited us to come here with her one Sunday. Honestly, we were pretty reluctant. You see, we've been all over the place and tried all sorts of things. We've done the bells and smells of high liturgy. We've done the anonymity of the megachurch scene. We've done fundamentalist churches where the preacher screamed at us about fornication for forty-five minutes. And the truth is we were worn out and fed up and about ready to give up on church for good. But . . . we love our friend, and she was so eager that we give this place a try, so we came along. Now, we've never been in a Reformed church before. In fact, I'm still not really sure what a Reformed church is. I hope you won't be offended if I tell you that we still find it a bit weird at times."

"But we've been here every week since she first brought us," Rachel says. "I'm not sure I totally understand why, but the approach to the Bible we've found here is beginning to fill a gaping hole in our spiritual lives. Having said that, we do have some questions and a few concerns. I mean, it's great that the pastor wants to explain whole books of the Bible, piece by piece, each week like that. I love it, don't get me wrong. But won't we miss out on some important practical guidance that we really need if that's all we get? And while I'm thinking about it, maybe having a praise service once in a while would lighten things up. I mean, I love the close study of the Bible and all, but it's pretty intense. Maybe we could have a Sunday of singing and prayers from time to time instead."

Steve looks thoughtful. "One of the things that is really striking about our worship here is that preaching is so central. Everything builds up to it. The pastor is always talking about 'the centrality of preaching.' And I like preaching. We're here for the preaching. But what about Communion? I wasn't really into the high liturgy we encountered at the Anglican and Lutheran churches we visited. But I must say their focus on the 'Eucharist,' as they called it, was really moving. There was such an air of mystery about it all, you know? I read somewhere that young people are looking for more of that these days. So maybe we need to downplay preaching just a little. Not too much, you understand, but enough to make room for a bit more ritual in our services."

Rachel chimes in again. "Another thing I don't get is why we insist on a monologue every week. I mean, the pastor is a fine communicator, but a bit more dialogue would go a long way. Maybe I'm the only one, but I've got to tell you honestly that after binge-watching Netflix till 1:30 a.m. the night before, I have a really hard time staying tuned in to a thirty-five-minute exposition of Leviticus! Maybe the sermon could be broken into shorter chunks and some video or drama added in between—just to help to hold our attention."

"Anyway, those are just a few thoughts on our experience here. I'd love to hear your feedback."

What should you say to Steve and Rachel? Clearly, they've been drawn to the approach to the preaching of the Word they've found at the church. Certainly, you will want to encourage them to stick with it and to give them some tools to help them to get the most out of it. And yet, there's still some confusion in their minds about what preaching is and about its place in the life of a Christian and in the worship of the church. They demonstrate an awareness that the "something more" they've been searching for is the exposition of the Scriptures. But there remains a gap between what they instinctively recognize they *need* and what years of broad evangelical church life has trained them to *want*.

Perhaps their questions mirror some of your own. You'd be quick to tell Steve and Rachel that being in a Reformed church has been a great blessing to you. And yet you'd have to admit that, while you've grown accustomed to how things are done, you've rarely asked *why* they're done that way. Presented with these thoughtful questions from a new family in the congregation, you are hard-pressed to know how best to answer them.

This book aims to be a short(ish!), one-stop shop for you *and* for Steve and Rachel. It's designed to establish the basic biblical and theological foundations for expositional preaching in a Reformed church, to highlight some historical examples, and to answer questions, fears, and objections people often have about preaching. This book is offered in the conviction that while we *do* need to equip pastors to preach the Word with faithfulness and urgency, we also need to equip those who hear the Word to profit from it. There are countless useful volumes for preachers about preaching. There are very few about preaching for those who listen to it. This is an attempt to begin to fill that gap.

The central question we're answering is this: In our digital, fast-paced information age, why should we center our Christian lives on the weekly reading and exposition of the Bible?

1

WHAT IS THE BIBLE?

Before we can come to grips with the *why* and the *how* of preaching, we need to consider the *what* of preaching. I'm going to argue that the complete text of the Old and New Testaments provides the *matter*, the basic *stuff*, of faithful preaching. But essential to making that case is a number of convictions about the nature of the Bible itself. Put a little differently, our deep belief in expositional preaching rests on an even deeper belief in the character of the Holy Scriptures. Our method is designed to honor the text because of the nature of the text itself.

What Kind of Book Is the Bible?

If the Bible were only a record of the best wisdom of the time, penned by a diverse and contradictory collection of ancient authors, we might well find it fascinating. We might even discover what we consider to be rich seams of ancient wisdom with which to inform our modern lives. But when it would come to the role such a book should play in the worship of the church or the life of a Christian, there would be no compelling reason that it should exert more influence than any other. We might even conclude that this book, far from offering fresh wisdom for modern problems, was out-of-date at best or downright offensive to contemporary sensibilities at worst. Perhaps the wisest thing to do with it would be to pick out those "inspirational" passages most acceptable to modern ears and to consign the rest to the rubbish heap of history, lest the Bible would prove itself to be the biggest liability for the church's success in reaching a new generation! We are happy to admit that on the presupposition that the Bible is nothing more than an ancient religious text, that would be a perfectly reasonable conclusion.

But that is not how the Bible speaks about itself. To be sure, the sixty-six books that comprise the canon of Scripture, penned over the span of about sixteen hundred years by an unknown number of human authors, are replete with cultural, historical, and stylistic diversity. But when the Bible speaks about itself, it is not primarily to the humanness of the authors that it directs our attention. This, it is assumed, is obvious and uncontroversial. ("*Of course* the Bible was written by an array of different people, from different backgrounds and personalities, for different purposes! So what?") Instead, when the Bible speaks about itself, it insists that, in addition to being the product of human culture, it is also at the same time the very Word of God.

In 2 Timothy 3:16 Paul says that "all Scripture is breathed out by God and profitable for teaching, for reproof, for correction, and for training in righteousness." The word translated *Scripture* here means something like "sacred writings," and in all fifty-one instances in which it appears in the New Testament, it refers to the Old Testament. Importantly, however, in two places the word *Scripture* refers to New Testament writings *alongside* the Old, indicating that the two share the same character and authority.

In 2 Peter 3:16, "the ignorant and unstable" are said to twist and distort the letters of Paul "as they do *the other Scriptures.*" Here Peter puts Paul's writings on a par with the Old Testament as belonging to the category of "Scripture." Similarly, in 1 Timothy 5:18, Paul quotes Deuteronomy 25:4 alongside the words of Jesus from Luke 10:7 and calls them both "Scripture." Paul clearly considers Jesus's words, recorded by Luke in his gospel, as sharing the same character as Moses's words in the Torah (an extraordinary claim for a Jew schooled, as was Paul, in rabbinic tradition). The Torah was given to Israel through Moses directly by God. Nothing carried greater authority for the Jewish people. And Paul places Jesus's words on par with it without a moment's hesitation.

To these two passages we might add many others that demonstrate the New Testament's knowledge that it is no mere human text. Consider 1 Corinthians 14:37 as an example. There Paul demonstrates his awareness that his teaching carries divine authority: "If anyone thinks that he is a prophet, or spiritual, he should acknowledge that the things I am writing to you are a command of the Lord." The Lord is addressing the Corinthians in Paul's writings.

So when 2 Timothy 3:16 says that "all Scripture is breathed out by God," we may safely apply "all Scripture" to the writings of both Testaments. The thirty-nine books of the Old and the twenty-seven of the New are alike "breathed out by God." That is to say, the words of the Bible are words spoken by God. Bible words are divine words. The Bible is the Word of God. Second Peter 1:20–21 even gives us some sense of *how* the Bible understands this to be so. "No prophecy of Scripture comes from someone's own interpretation. For no prophecy was ever produced by the will of man, but men spoke from God as they were carried along by the Holy Spirit." How was the Bible "breathed out by God"? The authors "were carried along by the Holy Spirit." "We could almost say they were *ferried* by the Spirit," writes Donald MacLeod. "Now when you're carried, you aren't led and you aren't prompted. There's a degree of passivity here: an emphasis on the controlling influence of the agent doing the carrying. In the production of Scripture God superintended and supervised the whole process, so that as the human agents thought and spoke and wrote, and as they used their sources, He was in control, setting them down at His own chosen destination and ensuring that they spoke exactly what He intended them to speak."[1]

There is, in other words, a beautiful compatibility at work here. The choices of the human authors and the divine superintendence of their every choice combine wonderfully, if mysteriously. The words and phrases, genres and styles, sources and influences that comprise the rich variety and texture of the Bible were all freely selected by its authors. God did not reduce them to automata, mere copyists to whom he dictated every word. Rather, he overruled in every circumstance that shaped the formation of their personalities and gifts. He governed the preoccupations and driving concerns that moved them to write. And he worked subtly to oversee and direct the writing of every word of every book of Holy Scripture. At no point was violence done to the will of the biblical author. And at no point did the biblical author fail to write only and exactly what God willed the author to write. Thus, these very human words are simultaneously and exhaustively the precise words God intends for us to know and the means by which he reveals himself and his will for us.

The fact that the whole Bible is the Word of God has a number of important implications.

Inerrancy

First, since the Bible is God's Word, it follows that it can be trusted completely. Since *God* cannot lie (see 2 Sam. 7:28; Titus 1:2; Heb. 6:18), it follows that God's *Word* cannot lie. It is without error and truthful in all that it teaches. The psalmist celebrated that fact with joyful abandon—and so should we.

> The law of the LORD is perfect,
>   reviving the soul;
> the testimony of the LORD is sure,
>   making wise the simple;
> the precepts of the LORD are right,
>   rejoicing the heart;
> the commandment of the LORD is pure,
>   enlightening the eyes;
> the fear of the LORD is clean,
>   enduring forever;
> the rules of the LORD are true,
>   and righteous altogether. (Ps. 19:7–9)

Authority

Second, since the Bible is the reliable Word of God, it carries the authority of God himself. There is an interesting incident in the gospel of John in which Jesus is accused of blasphemy. His answer reveals his understanding of the authority of the Bible.

> The Jews answered him, "It is not for a good work that we are going to stone you but for blasphemy, because you, being a man, make yourself God." Jesus answered them, "Is it not written in your Law, 'I said, you are

gods'? If he called them gods to whom the word of God came—and Scripture cannot be broken—do you say of him whom the Father consecrated and sent into the world, 'You are blaspheming,' because I said, 'I am the Son of God'?" (John 10:33–36)

Note *the way* Jesus argues. He appeals to the Word of God in Scripture that "cannot be broken." The Bible may not be violated. It has the force of absolute law. What the Bible says settles the matter. All Jesus need do is point to what "is written."

Along similar lines Jesus prayed to the Father on our behalf in John 17:17, "Sanctify them in the truth; your word is truth." He did not say merely, "Your word is truth*ful*." He said that the Word of God "*is truth*." Absolute truth, the truth of God, the truth according to which all other truth must conform, and by which it must be judged, has been sufficiently revealed for us in the Scriptures. The Bible is the *norma normans non normata*. It is the norm that norms all other norms but is not itself normed by any of them. Put a little differently, the Bible is the regulating principle, the owner's manual, the royal law of the great King of Kings. We are subject to the limits and rules of the Word of God; the Word of God is not subject to our private judgments and preferences.

Christian experience, personal prejudice, historic tradition, deeply held convictions—all must bow before the judgment of God in his Word. The Scriptures of the Old and New Testaments are the only infallible rule of faith and practice. As the Westminster Confession of Faith puts it, "The supreme judge by which all controversies of religion are to be determined, and all decrees of councils, opinions of ancient writers, doctrines of men, and private spirits, are to be examined, and in whose sentence we are to rest, can be no other but the Holy Spirit speaking in the Scripture."[2]

Sufficiency

Third, because the Bible is the Word of God, it is sufficient for us. The warning of Proverbs 30:5–6 is important here:

> Every word of God proves true;
> he is a shield to those who take refuge in him.
> Do not add to his words,
> lest he rebuke you and you be found a liar.

God has spoken his authoritative and reliable Word to us. We need no other, nor can we safely add to it in any way. What he has said is sufficient.

In Isaiah 8 the people of Judah were rebuked for seeking new revelations. They were consulting mediums. But God, through the prophet, summoned them back to the Bible: "To the teaching and to the testimony! If they will not speak according to this word, it is because they have no dawn" (v. 20). A neglect of the Bible in favor of extra revelation, or even the supposed discoveries of human reason, is an evidence that we "have no dawn"—that is, that we may still live in spiritual darkness.

As we have seen, Paul is utterly convinced that the Bible is sufficient for our every spiritual need: it is "profitable for teaching, for reproof, for correction, and for training in righteousness, that the man of God may be complete, equipped for every good work" (2 Tim. 3:16–17). There is no good work to which God might call us for which the Bible is not an adequate resource.

Clarity

Fourth, we must also insist that since the Bible is God's Word to us, it is marked by an essential clarity. Psalm 119:105 says that God's Word is "a lamp to my feet and a light to my path." The Scriptures are sufficiently clear to offer direction and illumination in all matters of belief or ethics. Deuteronomy 29:29 declares, "The secret things belong to the LORD our God, but the things that are revealed belong to us and to our children forever, that we may do all the words of this law." There are mysteries that remain hidden to us. But they are not our business. What is our business are the things God has revealed so that "we may do all the words of this law."

When we affirm the clarity of Scripture, we are not suggesting that every part is equally easy to understand or that each passage is equally significant for shaping our theology or equally relevant for directing our lifestyles. In 2 Peter 3:16, in the same breath as Peter calls Paul's writing "Scripture," he also admits that some of Paul's writings are "hard to understand." Isn't it encouraging (and ironic given how challenging his own writings are) that even the apostle Peter found Paul difficult? Not all of the Bible is equally clear. We're not pretending that Deuteronomy is easy for Western teenagers to understand and apply to their lives in high school, or that Revelation offers straightforward counsel to young mothers on how to raise children today (though no doubt there are important lessons for both groups from both these books). But while there are challenging portions of the Bible, we must insist that everything God wants us to know about himself, about sin and salvation, about ourselves and our world, and about how to live for his glory is either expressly set down in clear statements or can be deduced as necessary conclusions from the plain teaching of the Bible, so that no one who reads the Scriptures honestly can argue that God has not made his will for us apparent.

Christ Centered

Finally, the fact that the Bible is the Word of God means that it has a single unified message. Saint Augustine said that "the New is in the Old concealed, and the Old is in the New revealed."[3] The New Testament speaks about Christ as the one in whom the Old Testament finds fulfillment and to whom it constantly points us. In John 5:39, Jesus rebuked his Jewish opponents for searching the Scriptures, meaning the Old Testament, "because you think that in them you have eternal life; and it is they that bear witness about me." The Old Testament bears witness to Jesus Christ.

On the road to Emmaus in Luke 24, the risen Christ walked with two disciples who did not understand that Jesus had to suffer and rise again. Jesus said to them, "O foolish ones, and slow of heart to believe all that the prophets have spoken! Was it not necessary that the Christ should suffer these things and enter into his glory?" (vv. 25–26). And then, "beginning with Moses and all the Prophets, he interpreted to them in all the Scriptures the things concerning himself" (v. 27). All the Scriptures concern him.

Similarly, when the disciples were gathered in an upper room, Christ appeared to them and explained, "These are my words that I spoke to you while I was still with you, that everything written about me in the Law of Moses and the Prophets and the Psalms must be fulfilled" (Luke 24:44). The three divisions of the Hebrew Bible are listed here, each one speaking of his life, death, and resurrection. So Jesus taught that the Bible is a book about *him*. In prophetic promises of a coming Messiah, in the typology of temple and priesthood and sacrifice, in the unified structure of the unfolding covenants, the whole Bible hangs together with a single overarching story line, at the center of which stands the person and work of Jesus Christ. The Bible *must* be Christ centered, because as the Word of God, it points us to the only way of salvation for sinners. That way was provided in Jesus, to whom we have no other access apart from Scripture.

In summary, since the Bible is the Word of God, it must be *inerrant, authoritative, sufficient, clear,* and *Christ centered.* That means that this collection of ancient books is much more than a fascinating historical artifact, a record of ancient people and their varied religious experiences. It is the living Word for this and every generation. It is, as John Knox put it in the preface to the Scots Confession of 1560, "the mouth of God."[4]

The Centrality of Preaching in the Bible

But if all this is true, surely the reading and preaching of the Bible ought to occupy the primary place in our churches and in our Christian lives? Certainly, in the Bible itself that seems to have been the case, as the briefest survey of the biblical history will demonstrate.

In the Old Testament, preaching and teaching was central to the health of Israel. Aaron the priest was to teach God's statutes to the people (see Lev. 10:11). Moses prayed that the tribe of Levi would "teach Jacob your rules and Israel your law" (Deut. 33:10). When the Spirit of God came upon Azariah the son of Oded, he told King Asa of the need for reform in Judah because "for a long time Israel was without the true God, and without a teaching priest and without law" (2 Chron. 15:3). When Ezra the priest returned to Jerusalem after the exile, we are told that he had "set his heart to study the Law of the LORD, and to do it and to teach his statutes and rules in Israel" (Ezra 7:10). And in Nehemiah 8, we find Ezra doing just that. He read the law to the people from a "wooden platform" and, together with the Levites, explained and applied its message, "[giving] the sense, so that the people understood the reading" (Neh. 8:4, 7–8). The great writing prophets (for example, Isaiah, Jeremiah, Ezekiel, and Amos) certainly delivered the inspired oracles of God to the people, but they were also preachers of that message, proclaiming and applying it with force and urgency (see Ezek. 20:46; 21:2; Amos 7:16).

Importantly, we note that the dawn of the new covenant era was heralded by a great renewal of preaching. The dramatic ministry of John the Baptist was primarily a preaching ministry (see Matt. 3:1; Mark 1:7). Likewise, though accompanied by miraculous signs that witnessed to his divine authority and identity, Jesus understood his own ministry to be supremely a ministry of preaching. In Mark 1 he tells the disciples, "Let us go on to the next towns, that I may preach there also, for that is why I came out" (v. 38). And Mark adds, "He went throughout all

Galilee, preaching in their synagogues and casting out demons" (v. 39; see also Luke 4:43). Every Sabbath, Jesus customarily taught in the synagogues (see, for example, Matt. 4:23; 9:35; 13:54; Mark 6:2). When he appointed the twelve apostles, he sent them out to preach (see Mark 3:14), and when he had finished instructing them on their mission, he continued teaching and preaching in the surrounding towns (see Matt. 11:1).

In Luke 4:16–21, we even have an engaging example of Jesus's preaching ministry. In the synagogue at Nazareth, he read from the scroll of Isaiah 61:1–2:

> The Spirit of the Lord is upon me,
>   because he has anointed me
>   to proclaim good news to the poor.
> He has sent me to proclaim liberty to the captives
>   and recovering of sight to the blind,
> to set at liberty those who are oppressed,
>   to proclaim the year of the Lord's favor.
>   (Luke 4:18–19)

Then, sitting down in the customary posture of the synagogue teacher in those days, "he began to say to them, 'Today this Scripture has been fulfilled in your hearing'" (Luke 4:21). Presumably this is not all Jesus said. "He *began* to say . . ." seems to indicate that this is merely an apt summary of his startling message. Clearly he saw that this text described the nature of the mission entrusted to him: he came to proclaim good news. He had been given the Spirit of the Lord to empower him to preach. Rolling up the scroll, Jesus announced that the messianic prophecy he had just read was fulfilled before their eyes in him. Put simply, Jesus preached a Christ-centered expository sermon in which he *himself* was the living exposition of the text!

Furthermore, the Great Commission in Matthew 28:18–20 mandates that the church go into the world to make disciples, *teaching* all that Jesus commanded us. Teaching the Word of God is the way we are to make disciples. It is to be our great business as we obey our Savior's command. That is why, in obedience to this mandate, the apostles made preaching their constant priority throughout the book of Acts, and a glance at their Scripture-saturated sermons shows them all pointing to Christ. Paul gives us a sense of his own ministry priorities when he declared that "Christ did not send me to baptize but to preach the gospel, and not with words of eloquent wisdom, lest the cross of Christ be emptied of its power" (1 Cor. 1:17). Likewise, young Timothy was told to "preach the word; be ready in season and out of season" (2 Tim. 4:2).

This necessarily brief and incomplete survey of preaching in the Bible is surely enough to demonstrate that in both Testaments the exposition of Scripture was not peripheral to the welfare of the people of God. Because the Bible is what it is, the reading and preaching of the Scriptures took center stage in the ministry of the Levitical priests, in the work of the prophets, in the labors of John the Baptist, in the earthly ministry of Jesus, in the mandate given to the apostles, and in the priorities of Paul and Timothy. Preaching, at least in Bible times, was central, and that means, of course, that it still ought to be central today. And when it is, we ought not to be surprised to see the return of the same power that attended the church in the New Testament.

Shortly after Martyn Lloyd-Jones, famed for his commitment to expositional preaching, began his ministry at Aberavon in Wales, a reporter named Sam Jones came to hear him preach. "Mine was a human feeling of curiosity," he said. This mere curiosity was soon to change, however. Gripped by the preached Word in the midst of the congregation, he wrote, "Dr Lloyd-Jones has something to say . . . they are the words of one who has felt himself forced to speak by a greater than human power."[5] Lloyd-Jones's biographer, Iain Murray, concluded, "Sam Jones seems to have been one of the first to recognize in print that what was most unusual about the young preacher was not his change of career [Lloyd-Jones had given up a lucrative career in medicine to pursue gospel ministry] but his message itself and the manner in which it was delivered."[6] Lloyd-Jones abandoned all gimmicks, and soon, through the ordinary means of faithful preaching, God brought remarkable renewal and growth to his little church. His focus on preaching above all else caused quite a stir at the time. But why should it? That, after all, is the New Testament pattern, and it bore great fruit.

Reading the Bible with the Church

Given the New Testament pattern, each generation must engage with the text of Scripture afresh, and faithful preaching must bring the teaching of the Bible to bear upon the unique concerns and challenges of the day. But that does not mean that each new generation should try to read the Bible in a vacuum. One of the great slogans of the Reformation was *sola Scriptura*—the Bible alone. It was a call to let the Word of God rule in the life and teaching of the church. It was not, however, an encouragement to read the Bible—or preach the Bible—individualistically, in isolation from the history of the church. For two millennia, the church has been poring over the Scriptures and has provided a rich resource of interpretation and theological reflection. To neglect it is not wise.

The Bible is a big book. And, as we saw from 2 Peter 3:16, even during the lifetime of the apostolic authors, its meaning was often distorted and twisted by false teachers. Paul seems to recognize this problem when he urges his young protégé, Timothy, to "follow the pattern of the sound words that you have heard from me, in the faith and love that are in Christ Jesus" (2 Tim. 1:13). Through his preaching and personal training, Paul taught Timothy a body of doctrine to which they adhered, a pattern of sound words that expressed the teaching of Scripture. It was designed to ensure that when Timothy preached from one portion of Scripture, he did so in a way that was consistent with the teaching in the rest of Scripture, and thus the gospel itself would not suffer distortion. The history of biblical interpretation in general, together with the great creeds of the ancient church and the confessions of the magisterial Reformation in particular, continue to provide that pattern of sound words for us today. Frankly, as we hear the Scriptures taught in our churches, if, after two thousand years, no one else has taught what the preacher thinks he has discovered in the text of God's Word, the chances are he's got it wrong.

The principle of *sola Scriptura* (the Bible alone) does not call us to *nuda Scriptura* (the Bible only; the Bible without regard to the history of interpretation). We live at a time when radical autonomy and individualism are often equated with freedom. To be free, for many people, means to do things "my way." But to do things our own way does not reflect the impulse toward humility and teachability that the Bible itself produces in the hearts of all who love God and his Word. Surely, part of what it means to "honor [our] father and [our] mother" (Ex. 20:12) is to revere the wisdom of our fathers in the faith and to strive to read the Bible and teach the Bible *with the church* and not idiosyncratically.

To a significant degree, the genius of the Reformed tradition is its profound historical sensibility. It has always been concerned to restore Christian principles, piety, and practice to the simplicity of the pattern set by the ancient church. For example, during the Reformation Calvin worked to reform worship in Geneva in careful obedience to the Scriptures. Nevertheless, it is telling that he named his scripturally Reformed liturgy *The Form of Prayers and Hymns with the Manner of Administering the Sacraments and Consecrating Marriage according to the Custom of the Ancient Church.*[7] Calvin was determined that worship be regulated by the authority of the Word of God alone. *Sola Scriptura* was his governing principle. But that did not mean that worship, or preaching, or personal Christian living for that matter, should disregard the rich legacy of teaching from across the ages bequeathed to us by the church.

Furthermore, we need to listen not just to the history of biblical interpretation but to the living fellowship of the church today. As Sinclair Ferguson has pointed out, *sola Scriptura* "does not mean that God leaves us on our own. We discover the wonder of its truth not as isolated hermits but 'together with all the saints'!"[8] That is why preaching in the Reformed church plays such a central role. Private study, while important, does not occupy first place in our priorities. Small-group Bible study, as helpful as it can be, is not the primary venue of discipleship and spiritual nurture. Rather, in Reformed churches, preaching is the public, corporate engagement of the whole people of God with the Word of God through the pastors and elders called by God to shepherd the flock. We were never meant to treat the Bible as a loose collection of discreet texts—as "words from the Lord," ripped from their context, delivering atomized advice and encouragement for our individual needs. We are meant to read our Bibles in concert with the people of God—disciplined by their wisdom, helped by their insights, and sharpened in our understanding by those whom God has ordained to teach us.

The Preaching of the Word of God Is the Word of God

But why? What is happening when the Bible is read and preached like this? What ought we to expect from biblical preaching? What difference ought it to make to my life or yours? Romans 10:13–17 is one important passage that helps to answer those questions. In it Paul explains the need for evangelistic preaching, and there is a clear, logical progression in his argument. First he quotes Joel 2:32: "Everyone who calls on the name of the Lord will be saved" (Rom. 10:13). This articulates Paul's missionary objective. It is that more and more people will call on the name of the Lord and be saved. But faith is the vital instrument of salvation, and so he asks, "How then will they call on him in whom they have not believed?" (v. 14). If they are to call on him, they must have faith. They must believe. But, of course, the pressing question then becomes "How does God work this faith into the hearts of dead sinners? By what means will saving faith come to be in the hearts of the unconverted?"

Paul's response has enormous significance for our view of preaching. He asks, "How are they to believe in him of whom they have never heard? And how are they to hear without someone preaching?" (v. 14). Most English translations supply the word *of* here in order to clarify what translators assume Paul means: "How are they to believe in him *of* whom they have never heard?" But a more literal translation reads simply, "How are they to believe him *whom* they have not heard?"

Now it is true that in preaching we do indeed hear *of* Christ. We hear *about* him. We cannot hope to believe in a Jesus of whom we know nothing. But Paul is saying much more than that. It's not simply that we hear *of* him so that we are enabled to believe based on the relevant data. The point of preaching is not simply to communicate vital information about Jesus. No, Paul's point is that in faithful preaching *we hear Christ himself.* The living Christ, in the public exposition of the Word, is speaking to us.

Heinrich Bullinger, the Swiss reformer and contemporary of John Calvin, sums up Paul's point very well when he declares, "When this Word of God is now preached in the church by preachers lawfully called, we believe that the very Word of God is preached, and received of the faithful."[9] That is to say, God himself speaks—in Christ, by the Holy Spirit—and we hear his voice in faithful preaching. It is more than the mere communication of important information. Its potency lies in more than the rhetorical impact of the preacher's arguments or winning personality. The preaching of the Word *is* the Word. Paul commends the Thessalonians for grasping this point: "We also thank God constantly for this, that when you received the word of God, which you heard from us, you accepted it not as the word of men but as what it really is, the word of God, which is at work in you believers" (1 Thess. 2:13). Similarly, Peter reminds his readers in Asia Minor that "whoever speaks" must speak "oracles of God" (1 Peter 4:11). In our faithful speaking of the Word of God, God speaks. The preaching of the Word of God is the Word of God.

Many Christians today long to hear from God. Sadly, they look to hear him speak in all sorts of mystical ways—in new revelations, in ecstatic experiences, in dreams and visions and inexplicable encounters—not realizing that week by week, when the Bible is opened and proclaimed, we hear the voice of God. We needn't go searching for the extraordinary and the mysterious. Though preaching may *appear* ordinary and mundane, in it the voice that caused light to shine out of darkness at the dawn of creation causes the light of the knowledge of the glory of God to shine in our hearts in the face of Jesus Christ (see 2 Cor. 4:6). The Christ who called Lazarus from death by his mere word and summons (see John 11:43) speaks to us still in the preached Word!

Questions for Further Reflection

1. In your view, how should the authority, reliability, sufficiency, and Christ-centeredness of the Bible affect preaching?
2. What does it mean to read the Bible with the church across the ages? Why is this an important safeguard against error?
3. How does it change the way you listen to preaching to know that, when the sermon faithfully explains and applies what the written Word of God says, the sermon itself is the Word of God to you?

2

WHY EXPOSITIONAL PREACHING?

My contention is not only that preaching should derive its *warrant*, its authorization, from the *commands* of Scripture—the Bible clearly commands preaching, after all[1]—but that preaching should also derive its *form*, its basic method and shape, from the *character* of Scripture. Since the Bible is the Word of God—inerrant, authoritative, sufficient, clear, and centered on Christ—the task of the preacher must be to say what the text of the Word of God says and no more. Puritan William Perkins put it plainly: "The Word of God alone is to be preached, in its perfection and inner consistency. Scripture is the exclusive subject of preaching, the only field in which the preacher is to labor."[2]

The preacher must illustrate the truths he finds in the Bible so that people can understand them, and he must apply what is being said in the text so people can live in light of it. But in all this, at every point, it is the text preached, not the preacher's whim or the hearer's concerns, that govern how the Bible is proclaimed.

This is what we mean when we talk about expositional preaching. David Helm defines *expositional preaching* as "empowered preaching that rightfully submits the shape and emphasis of the sermon to the shape and emphasis of a biblical text. . . . It brings out of the text what the Holy Spirit put there . . . and does not put into the text what the preacher thinks might be there."[3]

Expositional preaching should demonstrate a deep respect for the text of the Bible as its sole authority. Not only the *content* but the *contours* of the sermon should bow submissively to the rule of the Word. As P. T. Forsyth has put it, "The great reason why the preacher must return continually to the Bible is that the Bible is the greatest sermon in the world. Above every other function, the Bible is a sermon. . . . It is the preacher's book because it is the preaching book."[4]

The Bible is God addressing his world. It is, as Forsyth suggests, God's sermon. Exposition is simply the business of unpacking the content of that divine proclamation. Reformed convictions about the nature of the biblical text should therefore lead to an approach to preaching in Reformed churches that privileges exposition. "This approach," writes Tim Keller, "testifies that you believe every part of the Bible to be God's Word, not just the particular themes and not just the parts you feel comfortable agreeing with. . . . A sustained expository approach over time—in which you take care to draw out the meaning of each text, to ground all your assertions in the text, and to move through large chunks of the Bible systematically—will best pass your confidence in the Scriptures along to your listeners."[5]

That's not to say that expositional preaching is simply a running commentary on the text, as if all that is needed is to give explanations of words and phrases and sentences and paragraphs and little else. This would be to reduce the sermon to something like a lecture and would ultimately dishonor the text it seeks to serve by being far too dull and lifeless to serve adequately as the urgent proclamation of good news for the world. Sinclair Ferguson is right when he insists that the function of an expositional sermon "is not limited to furnishing information. Rather, it is dominated by a message, and is intended to produce action as well as to impart instruction. Indeed, precisely because this is a function of the teaching of Scripture (grace leads to faith, indicatives lead to imperatives), it is also necessarily a dimension of exegetical preaching."[6]

Good preaching is the servant of the Bible's text, and this means that it serves not only to convey the text's meaning but to accomplish its ends. Good preaching seeks to do in the heart of the hearer what the Bible aims to do. It has as its target the transformation of the life, not only the education of the mind. After all, the message of the Bible is electrifying. But a mere running commentary will be as much use in conducting that electricity as a brick. A well-crafted sermon that explains, illustrates, and applies the text in a form that serves the agenda of the text and the welfare of the hearer is the right conductor for the current of divine power.

In short, the nature of the Bible itself *demands* exposition. But there are doubtless many additional reasons to privilege expository preaching above all other forms. In what follows, I offer eleven arguments in favor of expositional preaching.

Expositional Preaching Honors God by Respecting How He Has Revealed Himself to Us

God did not give us a collection of aphorisms. The Bible is not a compendium of arcane knowledge or mystic ritual. God has not provided a rule book for life, offering step-by-step guidance on what to do in every conceivable circumstance. The Bible is really a *library*. It is a collection of books that display artistry and literary skill. It is composed of history, poetry, and case law. It contains proverbs and parables, allegories and apocalypses. It is a collection of gospel accounts based on eyewitness testimony and letters addressing theology and ethics. It sings and celebrates, laments and loves. It is diverse and cohesive, multifaceted and laser-focused on a single grand story.

To preach the Bible faithfully, then, must mean more than simply to use the text for our own ends. It requires attention to the literary genre, the historical context, the grammar and syntax, the flow of argument, the arc of the narrative. It requires us to slow down and see what is there, on its own terms, and begin to understand what the text must have meant to its original hearers before we can begin to understand what it means to us. This is the work of exposition. Nothing less honors the text in all its complexity, and that is why nothing else adequately respects the Lord who speaks to us in it.

Expositional Preaching Highlights the Coherence and Unity of the Bible

Expositional preaching will ordinarily seek to engage with large portions of the biblical text, even whole Bible books, over several weeks. But on those occasions when stand-alone sermons are preached, or when sermon series follow a topical theme rather than move through whole Bible books sequentially, these too must still be expositional in method and form. Good topical preaching does not use the text as a hook on which to hang the preacher's theme so that the text becomes incidental to the message. Instead, even a topical sermon in an expository mode will identify a text that legitimately addresses the subject in hand and will work to help us to understand the unique way in which this particular text addresses that particular subject, so that the text, not the theme, still rules the sermon.

But all faithful exposition, whether topical or sequential, must read the passage to be preached in light of its context and in connection with the unfolding story line of the Bible as a whole, leading us, ultimately, to the gospel of Jesus Christ. This approach to preaching means that, in a sense, every sermon is a whole-Bible sermon. A good expositional sermon will point out the Old Testament background to New Testament ideas or lead you to New Testament fulfillment from Old Testament promises. Christian preachers must preach the whole Bible as Christian Scripture.

So if the text is in the Old Testament, the preacher must preach it as the Bible that Christ preached and Paul preached as they proclaimed the coming of the kingdom in the arrival of Jesus of Nazareth. If the text is in the New Testament, the preacher must preach it as the heir of the prophets, addressing the children of Abraham, the people of the covenant promise (see Gal. 3:29). The church is the Israel of God, "a chosen race, a royal priesthood, a holy nation, a people for his own possession" (1 Peter 2:9; see also Deut. 7:6).

That means that the Old and New Testaments belong to us and really make sense only when read and explained together, each in light of the other. In my judgment, the best way for preaching to demonstrate how the whole Bible fits together, with a single, coherent message and story line, is to work systematically through large portions of the text, highlighting the internal connections, citations, allusions, and trajectories that always eventually lead to the good news about Jesus.

Expositional Preaching Best Promotes the Work of Christian Formation

It has been said that it takes a whole Bible to preach a whole Christ to make a whole Christian. Systematic expositional preaching challenges the temptation we all feel to stick to the easy texts and the familiar Bible books. It recognizes that the promotion of spiritual maturity demands exposure to the complete array of biblical material. While not every text is equally clear or equally applicable in every circumstance, nevertheless every text has been "breathed out by God and [is] profitable" (2 Tim. 3:16). Not only the gospel accounts and the letters of Paul but the genealogies and Mosaic case law have their lessons. While the Psalms speak to our hearts so readily, the prophetic oracles against Edom or Babylon are not without their message for today's hearer. The practicality of the Proverbs gives light in our search for guidance, but the often obscure instructions for the building of the tabernacle also have a role in helping us to see something of God's concern for his glory and our good.

Showing Christ in the whole Bible is God's way of making us whole Christians, because it stretches our thinking and takes us to hard texts and strange stories. Sustained exposure to the systematic exposition of the entire Bible over time confronts us with the full scope not only of biblical truth but of human experience as well.

Tragedy, sin, doubt, fear, hope, love, grief, joy, and every other dimension of our complex inner life is brought to light and examined in the Word of God, and the good news about Jesus is applied to it all for our conversion and comfort.

Expositional Preaching Shows That the Power Is in the Word

In Mark 4, Jesus tells a parable about a farmer who scatters seed on the ground:

> He sleeps and rises night and day, and the seed sprouts and grows; he knows not how. The earth produces by itself, first the blade, then the ear, then the full grain in the ear. But when the grain is ripe, at once he puts in the sickle, because the harvest has come. (vv. 27–29)

The parable tells us about the nature of the kingdom of God. It grows, although the sower "knows not how." His task is to scatter the seed. He does not cause the growth. Having sown the seed, the farmer is passive. There *is* kingdom work to be done, to be sure. The seed *must* be scattered. The Word *must* be preached. But in Jesus's story, the ripening harvest of changed lives is not the result of anything the farmer does.

We must have confidence in the kingdom that grows "by itself." The life is in the seed, not in the sower. When preaching is expositional, it signals to all who listen to it that the life is in the seed, that power for lasting change is not to be looked for in the brilliant insights of the preacher but in the meaning and implications of the Word. The Bible is the comprehensive provision of God for the spiritual needs of his people (see 2 Tim. 3:16–17). Faithful exposition aims to drive every nose into the Bible because *that* is where the power lies.

Paul writes in 1 Corinthians 1 that the "the word of the cross is folly to those who are perishing, but to us who are being saved it is the power of God" (v. 18). He reminds the Corinthians that "it pleased God through the folly of what we preach [perhaps better translated 'through the folly of *preaching*'] to save those who believe" (v. 21). Expositional preaching especially highlights the Word of the cross—which is the burden of the whole Bible—as the saving power of God. Expositional preaching leaves us in no doubt that when someone comes to saving faith in Jesus, they have not been swayed or brainwashed or manipulated into it by the charismatic personality or rhetorical techniques of the pastor. Expositional preaching is "Bible-forward" preaching: those who come to trust in Christ under such a ministry do not look to the church's leadership for assurance of salvation or spiritual sustenance but to the Scriptures that those leaders proclaim.

Expositional Preaching Submits to the Authority of the Word

In our relativistic age, when truth claims are viewed with immediate suspicion, there is wisdom in allowing the ancient text of the sixty-six books of the Bible to speak. In doing so, we show that our message submits to an authority beyond our tradition or our taste. But "this is unclear in sermons that touch lightly on Scripture and spend most of the time in stories, lengthy arguments, or thoughtful musings. The listener might easily wiggle out from under the uncomfortable message by thinking, *Well, that's just your interpretation.*"[7]

Faithful preaching in Reformed churches doesn't aim to provide peppy TED Talks on uplifting life issues. It's not concerned to philosophize or sway crowds with beautiful prose. It's not performance art. Neither should faithful preaching in Reformed churches display the learning and brilliance of the pastor, leaving average church members to think they could never hope to understand the Bible for themselves, much less explain it to someone else, without degrees in theology and biblical languages. A faithful Reformed preacher believes that Christ the King exercises his authority over him and over the church through the Scriptures. He is called to proclaim only what the King has said in his authoritative Word, and he is to do it in such a way that displays the authority of Christ, not the authority of historic traditions or the latest pop-cultural insights or his personal education. Submission to the authority of Christ means submission to the authority of the Bible. That submission is expressed best in preaching that attends closely to the text of Scripture itself. It is expositional.

Expositional Preaching Offers Respite from the Concerns and Burdens of the World

Faithful exposition should face squarely the concerns of the flock and not dodge matters of cultural moment and urgency. But the news media should not set the agenda for the church and certainly not for the pulpit. Preachers can feel an enormous pressure to keep up with the culture and speak to the great issues of the day. We want to feel relevant and to know that our messages are welcomed. One way to do that is to give people each Sunday a sermon designed to speak to their fears and foibles. Using this model, the pastor can soon fall under the tyranny of keeping up, always trying to stay abreast of the latest cultural trend. But the church's calling is to be not a venue for social commentary but an embassy of the kingdom of heaven.

In 1946 James S. Stewart addressed with some urgency the drive felt by the preachers of his generation to speak to the latest news in a way that continues to resonate today: "It is deplorable that God's hungry sheep, hoping for the pasture of the living Word, should be fed on disquisitions on the themes of the latest headlines.

It is calamitous that men and women, coming up to the church on a Sunday—with God only knows what cares and sorrows, what hopes and shadowed memories, what heroic aspirations and moods of shame burdening their hearts—should be offered nothing better for their sustenance than one more dreary diagnosis of the crisis of the hour."[8]

Expositional preaching may apply the Word to the particular cultural moment as necessary. The preacher may illustrate the message of the text by appealing to the latest news and events. But when you sit in the pew, there is relief—*refuge* even—in the knowledge that whatever voices are competing for your attention on TV and social media this week, *here* in the church of Jesus Christ you will hear the voice of God speaking good news to your heart in his unchanging Word.

Expositional Preaching Models
How to Read the Bible

Preaching shapes those who listen to it, not just by what is being taught but, over time, by the *way* in which it is taught. When preachers give weight to the authority of Scripture and devote themselves to understanding the details of each text and the scope of the whole, they train their hearers to do the same. Faithful exposition works to avoid imposing meanings upon the text. It strives to avoid spiritualizing or reducing historical narrative to an arbitrary allegory. It shuns proof texts and mystical "words from the Lord" that care nothing for literary context. It nails the spiritual and ethical and doctrinal and pastoral and evangelistic burdens of the preacher and the hearers to the text itself. Furthermore, it disciplines us to patiently listen to God in his Word in the confidence that if we simply follow the teaching that is already there, rather than rush on to our own preoccupations and priorities, we will find the wisdom we need. The preacher is not just a Bible teacher and an evangelist and a pastor in the pulpit. He is also a model Bible reader. Regularly sitting under consistent scriptural exposition trains our interpretive muscles, informs our instincts as readers, and equips us to read both responsibly and profitably.

Expositional Preaching Guards against Hobby Horses

Nothing can prevent a preacher with enough will and creativity from insisting on his hobby horses. John Stott retells the story of the Baptist preacher "who had such pronounced views about baptism that he simply could not leave the subject alone. One morning he announced his text, 'Adam, where art thou?' He then continued, 'There are three lines we shall follow. First, where Adam was; secondly, how he was to be got from where he was; and thirdly and lastly, a few words about baptism.' "[9] Even the best preachers are tempted to emphasize their favored subjects or to skip over the hard texts! But systematic expositional preaching *does* impose some much-needed discipline upon the pulpit and the preacher . . . and on the congregation too for that matter. After all, we may want our pet subjects addressed. We may believe that our priorities ought to be the priorities of every sermon (and of every other church member). But when preacher and hearer alike learn to submit themselves to the text, and the next, and to the one after that, we are spared from imbalance and idiosyncrasy. Peter Adam put it well when he said, "Expository sermons help us to let God set the agenda for our lives. The danger of topical preaching is that it implies that we know what is important! Expository preaching lets God set the agenda in an obvious and public way."[10]

Expositional Preaching Bonds Pastor and Flock over Time

The slow-food movement is a fad that developed in reaction to the unhealthy fast-food industry. It emphasizes growing and raising food organically. It highlights the connections between how we produce food, how good it can taste, and how healthful it can be. It highlights the virtue of slowing down and getting involved in the production, cultivation, and consumption of real food, well made.

There is a sense in which biblical exposition is spiritual slow food. Expositional preaching, we might say, is a slow-discipleship method. To be sure, each sermon on its own can be revolutionary in the life of a Christian. Dramatic progress in Christian discipleship is often made as God works through a single message. But generally speaking, expositional preaching bears most fruit as a result of prolonged exposure of a congregation to the Scriptures, Sunday by Sunday, verse by verse, over extended periods of time. Consistently sitting under this kind of faithful preaching slowly cultivates healthy appetites and develops spiritual taste buds for the things that really count. It presses the preacher and the hearer toward one another as they grow together in faithful commitment. Over time the preacher learns the needs of his flock so that he is able, more and more, to pastor them in his preaching, applying the text with precision and care for their spiritual welfare. And over time the congregation becomes attuned to the preacher's unique gifts and personality and pulpit manner, so their ability to digest the diet he provides grows and grows. In this way, faithful expositional preaching cultivates the bond between the pastor and the flock and brings both the preacher and the hearer together in the discipleship process.

Expositional Preaching Follows the Best Examples of Christian History

Throughout history there have been outstanding examples of expositional preaching that bear eloquent testimony to the fruitfulness of this approach to the ministry of the

Word. A sketch of three notable examples must suffice to make the point.

John Chrysostom (ca. 347–407)

The best-known preacher of the early church, John Chrysostom, was called "Golden Mouth" for his oratorical brilliance. He was a devoted expositor and pastor of the people. Hughes Oliphant Old notes that during his ministry in Antioch and then in Constantinople, Chrysostom preached almost daily, each sermon picking up from the place in Scripture where he had stopped the day before. In addition to many occasional topical sermons, Chrysostom has left the church sixty-seven sermons on Genesis, fifty-eight on selected psalms, ninety on Matthew, eighty-eight on John, fifty-five on Acts, thirty-four on Hebrews, and more than two hundred on the letters of Paul.[11] He carefully studied each text of Scripture in advance and clearly prepared his message with great forethought, though he spoke extemporaneously. The written record of his sermons, taken down by a stenographer as they were preached, still bear the marks of spoken oratory rather than literature.

Chrysostom was a sober exegete, unwilling to allegorize or spiritualize the text beyond its plain meaning. This didn't mean that he failed to preach Christ from the Old Testament, however. In a sermon on Genesis 22—the famous account of Abraham sacrificing Isaac—Chrysostom made the connection to the cross explicit:

"All this, however, happened as a type of the Cross."[12] In his systematic exposition, he preached Christ from the whole Bible. It's also important to note that he was not afraid to be direct in his application of the message to the consciences of his hearers. In one sermon, he rebuked those who had skipped church to attend horse races at the hippodrome![13] It seems that preaching had to compete with sports and leisure as much then as it does today.

John Calvin (1509–1564)

The preaching of John Calvin is another example of a sustained pulpit ministry characterized by sequential biblical exposition. Famously, Calvin was expelled from Geneva in 1538. He preached his last sermon on Easter day. When he was invited back in September 1541, he climbed the pulpit steps at St. Pierre's church and opened the Bible at the place he had broken off three years before. He said, "I took up the exposition where I had stopped, indicating by this that I had only temporarily interrupted my office of preaching and not given it up entirely."[14] From the year 1549 onward, Calvin preached every morning, Monday to Friday, on alternate weeks, and twice on Sundays, with a single sermon on Wednesdays in the intervening weeks, at St. Pierre's. Each sermon lasted approximately an hour and moved, verse by verse, through whole books of the Bible.

On the alternate weeks when he was not preaching daily, Calvin lectured on theology three times a day, and every Friday evening he provided a lecture at a citywide Bible study.[15] The weekday sermons covered Old Testament texts, and Sundays were reserved for the exposition of the New Testament. In this way, he preached nearly four thousand sermons (more than 170 a year), covering almost the entire Bible in the course of his ministry. "He began at chapter one verse one of a book and continued with one or a few or many verses for each sermon until he had got to the end of that book. Then the next day or the next Sunday he started on another book."[16]

Commenting on Calvin's desire to bring the truth of the text to bear on his hearers' consciences, John Gerstner says that "he was so eager to get at application that he often introduced it in the midst of the exposition. In other words, application was the dominant element in the preaching of John Calvin to which all else was subordinated."[17] Far from being a dusty academic preacher, Calvin was a shepherd and a prophet and a herald of the truth of God for his generation. His ministry exemplified expositional care, deep learning, and profound love for Christ and his church. His sermons are full of Christ and full of application and continue to shape the church to this day.

D. Martyn Lloyd-Jones (1899–1981)

Lloyd-Jones fulfilled an influential preaching ministry, first at Sandfields Chapel in Aberavon, Wales, and then at the historic Westminster Chapel in central London. He preached sequentially through books of the Bible on

Sunday mornings and on Friday evenings and delivered expositional sermons from individual passages with an evangelistic edge on Sunday evenings. During the week, he travelled extensively throughout Britain to preach and teach. His sermons on Romans, Ephesians, and the Sermon on the Mount, among others, continue to be in print and have exercised an enormous influence over the evangelical and Reformed church. J. I. Packer describes "the Doctor's" preaching as electrifying: "Combining the electric energy of the orator with the analytic precision of the courtroom or the clinic, and focusing his business-like rhetoric on the inner drama of the gracious hound of heaven capturing and changing sinners' benighted hearts, he communicated an overwhelming sense of the greatness of God and the weight of spiritual issues."[18]

Lloyd-Jones believed in rigorous doctrinal exposition in the pulpit and was unashamed to be theological in his preaching. "What is preaching?" he asked in his famous lectures on preaching. His answer demonstrates that, for Lloyd-Jones, there was nothing dreary or boring about faithful expositional preaching:

> What is preaching? Logic on fire! Eloquent reason! Are these contradictions? Of course they are not. Reason concerning this Truth ought to be mightily eloquent, as you see it in the case of the Apostle Paul and others. It is theology on fire. And a theology which does not take fire, I maintain, is a defective theology; or at least

the man's understanding of it is defective. Preaching is theology coming through a man who is on fire. A true understanding and experience of the Truth must lead to this. I say again that a man who can speak about these things dispassionately has no right whatsoever to be in a pulpit; and should never be allowed to enter one.[19]

The marriage of "theology on fire" and sequential exposition of the text was the hallmark of his ministry. But he had no time for the idea that a running commentary is the same thing as expository preaching: "People say, 'It is biblical.' It is not. Biblical preaching brings out a message. A mechanical explanation of the meaning of words—not fused into a message with point and power that leaves hearers glorying in God—is not preaching. It is not enough to make an affirmation of Christian truth; it may be heard as just one view against another. *We have got to bring a message.*"[20]

This is what we mean by expositional *preaching*. It is possible to have exposition without preaching. However, it is not possible to have preaching without exposition. Preaching is more than mere exposition. It is, as Lloyd-Jones put it, a message with point and power. There is fire, a sense of the weight of God speaking in his Word.

Chrysostom, Calvin, and Lloyd-Jones were all engaged in careful, systematic expositional preaching. And yet let it be remembered that all three brought their personalities and temperaments to the task. Each lived in a unique time confronted by challenges that were specific to their contexts. Their method was essentially the same, but they would have sounded different.

Lloyd-Jones's Welsh brogue and solemn demeanor lent gravity to his preaching. He typically began slowly, his tone deliberate and his pace measured. But as he warmed to the message, his words would flow with increasing speed, and his voice would rise in urgency and volume.[21]

Calvin was by temperament and training a scholar of the classics and of law. He preferred a cloistered life of academic pursuit and was so reluctant to take up the task of preaching and pastoring that his colleague, William Farel, had to utter a "dreadful imprecation" to persuade him.[22] Yet the transcripts of his sermons demonstrate preaching that was marked by extraordinary pastoral wisdom and often by great courage, as he pursued the reformation of the Genevan church.

Chrysostom was often called "Golden Mouth" because of the soaring rhetoric that marked his preaching. He held his audiences spellbound.

The work of expositional preaching needn't flatten personalities, neither does it demand similarity in language, tone, composition, or rhetorical style. It is simply the expression of a profound commitment to let the text of the Holy Scriptures govern the content and message of a sermon. It was this commitment that marked the greatest preachers in history as they harnessed their gifts and temperaments in the service of the gospel.

Expositional Preaching Meets Our Need to Know Christ

So why do we need our pastors to preach expositionally? We need them to because our great need as Christians is to hear from God. Nothing ensures that the message of the sermon conforms to the message of the text like careful exposition. The myriad voices that clamor for our attention every day push and pull at us with a dizzying array of competing opinions. Our inner voices of conscience and conviction, memory and ambition, desire and regret often are distorted or incorrect. When preaching faithfully expounds the text of Holy Scripture, applying its truth to our hearts and lives, we finally hear the one voice that really matters. God, in Christ, by the Holy Spirit speaking in the Word, exposes our sin, speaks comfort and consolation to us, summons us to new obedience, informs our consciences, and directs our convictions. He cuts through the din of mere human opinion (including the preacher's own!) and directs our steps in the way everlasting.

What's more, when exposition takes place sequentially, week after week, through extended sections of the Bible, a cumulative effect develops. Slowly, we learn how to read the Bible for ourselves. We have the delightful, and sometimes uncomfortable, surprise of discovering that very often in preaching God provides for our deepest soul needs, as the exposition speaks to our questions and concerns, sometimes in startling demonstrations of divine serendipity. The secrets of our hearts are laid bare. Our unruly desires are disciplined by the Word of God. In short, regular exposure to the systematic exposition of the whole Bible forms and shapes us more effectively than anything else ever can. This best comports with the teaching of the Bible itself. And this, too, meets the deepest need of our hearts—to know Christ.

Questions for Further Reflection

1. How does expositional preaching help you to read and understand the Bible better for yourself?
2. When so many voices compete for our attention, in what ways does it reassure us to see how a sermon clearly arises from the text of Holy Scripture?
3. Listening to expositional preaching can be demanding. Why is that a good thing? What fruit will it bear in our Christian lives over time?

3

EXPOSITIONAL PREACHING AND THE MINISTRY OF THE CHURCH

When you attend a Reformed church, one distinctive you will quickly identify is the central place of preaching in the life of the congregation. It stands at the heart of the Reformed approach to the three core ministries entrusted to us: worship, evangelism, and Christian discipleship. In this chapter we will look at how preaching relates to each of these themes. Of course, the centrality of preaching in a Reformed church contrasts, sometimes starkly, with the place of expositional preaching in other traditions.

In many churches, worship centers on music or liturgy. In some churches, preaching is almost viewed as a potential distraction or hindrance to worship—one that should be suspended at times so that the congregation can engage in prolonged seasons of singing and prayer, often in pursuit of deeper spiritual experience (which, it is assumed, preaching can never supply). In other churches, preaching is at best preparatory for the main event, which is the celebration of the Eucharist, and so should be kept as brief as possible. The furniture of the church building has been arranged to reflect the central importance of the eucharistic celebration, with the pulpit to the side and the altar at the center.

But in Reformed churches, preaching is both the center and the high point of worship.

When it comes to evangelism, the last thing many of us would think to do is bring a friend to hear *preaching*. We may have been trained to witness to our friends. Perhaps we've memorized a short gospel presentation or a collection of Bible verses to use in evangelistic conversations. Small-group discussion has become a popular venue for evangelistic engagement in a nonthreatening environment. But preaching is heavy. It is scary. And it likely won't make any sense to our non-Christian friends.

But in Reformed churches, preaching is God's primary instrument of evangelism.

The focal point of Christian nurture and growth for many today, especially as exemplified in evangelical parachurch ministries, is small group and one-on-one discipleship programs. A mentoring relationship is vital. An accountability group is key. Meeting with an intimate circle of Christian friends for biblical study and prayer is the engine that will drive your growth as a believer. But preaching is hit-and-miss. It may or may not scratch where you itch. Attend church because it is your duty as a Christian, by all means. But you can go so much deeper in your small group.

But in Reformed churches, preaching is the principle means of discipleship.

To be clear, Reformed churches have a high view of the sacraments and prize the celebration of the Lord's Supper. The liturgy of the church matters to us. And we celebrate and encourage the work of every Christian as he or she shares the good news about Jesus with friends and family. Small groups have always been valuable tools to further our fellowship and mutual encouragement in the faith. But in the Reformed tradition, preaching takes center stage, while liturgy, sacraments, personal evangelism, and small groups all play supporting roles. Not the other way around.

These three themes—worship, evangelism, and discipleship—summarize the church's calling in the world. These are our divinely ordained priorities. Our task is to glorify God, to reach the world with the gospel, and to nurture believers into maturity. For the Reformed, the Word of God preached is the primary means by which these objectives are to be realized because we believe God has made it the priority.

Preaching and Worship

Often, we conceive of worship more narrowly than we ought. For us, too often, worship is singing—or the joyous *feeling* of adoration as we are caught up in the atmosphere generated by the music and lyrics. To the question

"How was church today?" we might answer, "It was great; I was able *really to worship* this morning." Worship is an aspiration—something we aim to experience but do not always achieve. This way of thinking is sometimes reflected in the words of the "worship leader" who begins the service, saying, "In a little while Pastor John will come and talk to us from the Bible. But first we are going to have a time of worship. Close your eyes and shut everyone out. It's just you and Jesus!"

But this is to sever the vital union of praise and proclamation, preaching and prayer, the voice of God to us and the voice of our response to him. It is to suggest that worship is mainly *our* activity and biblical instruction is something secondary. In the Bible, however, worship—both the activity and the feeling of reverent wonder and adoration—is the product of the truth of God in the hearts and minds of those who hear it. John Piper has argued that "worship in the New Testament, compared to worship in the Old Testament, moved toward a focus on something radically simple and inward, with manifold external expressions in life and liturgy that could be adapted over the centuries in thousands of different cultures. Worship in the New Testament took on the character suited for a *go-tell* religion for all nations (Matt. 28:18–20), as opposed to the detailed rituals prescribed in the Old Testament suited for a *come-see* religion (1 Kings 10:1–13)."[1]

In other words, since New Testament worship has the character of a "*go-tell* religion," the proclamation of the Word is at its very heart and gives it its characteristic shape. When Paul exhorts the Corinthian church about their misuse of the gift of tongues, he calls them to ensure that whenever tongue speakers exercise their gift it is accompanied by an interpretation (see 1 Cor. 14:23–25). The priority is to clearly communicate God's truth for the good of others rather than to use gifts for indulgent self-expression. Paul asks us to suppose that when the church gathers a non-Christian is always present. If everyone is speaking an unintelligible language, "will [visitors] not say that you are out of your minds?" (v. 23). But if a visiting unbeliever hears the intelligible and authoritative communication of the inspired Word of God—what happens then? "He is convicted by all, he is called to account by all, the secrets of his heart are disclosed, and so, falling on his face, he will worship God and declare that God is really among you" (vv. 24–25).

What is the result when the Word of God is faithfully proclaimed? It penetrates hearts and consciences. It exposes sin and applies the gospel remedy. And it results in worship, for it brings us into a direct encounter with the living God himself, who is dealing with us by his Word. For Paul the goal of intelligibly communicating the Word in the gathered assembly of the church is *worship*.

But we are not just arguing that worship *results* from the preaching of the Word. We are arguing that biblical preaching itself *is* worship. It is an act of worship commanded by the Word of God.[2] As such, the central place of preaching in our services highlights the fact that in worship, God moves toward us first. We are there to meet with him and to hear from him and to be dealt with by him, under his Word and by his Spirit; only secondarily and reflexively are we there to offer sacrifices of praise and thanksgiving. Worship is not just our response to God. It is first God's invitation to us to commune with him.

As Sinclair Ferguson notes, in faithful preaching, "God speaks through His word, from His heart to His people's hearts, as surely as if His voice is heard. Thus, the deepest sense of worship is intended to take place during and because of preaching. It is in this way that the most interior soul engagement with the Lord is ordinarily to be experienced and the profoundest responses of praise evoked. . . . Worship and preaching, therefore, belong together. Through the ministry of the Spirit, preaching is worship and also evokes worship."[3]

Preaching is doxological. It is first of all for God. God is exalted in the publication of his name and his glories, his mighty acts and his manifold mercies. In 2 Corinthians 2, Paul speaks about his own preaching ministry. He highlights the immensity of what is at stake. Eternal destinies are being worked out in response to his gospel proclamation. Among those who are perishing, it is "a fragrance from death to death," and among those who are being saved, it is "a fragrance from life to life" (v. 16). As people hear the good news about Jesus and respond, the great issue of eternity is settled. But before his preaching was the fragrance of life or death to his unconverted human hearers, Paul tells us that it was first "the aroma of Christ *to God*" among them (v. 15). God "smells" the sweet perfume of Christ in the preaching of the gospel, and it brings him honor. Paul was preaching to the lost not just for the sake of their salvation. He was preaching to the lost *for the pleasure of God*. His preaching was for God's sake, for his glory. He preached for the smile of the Father as he spread the fragrance of his Son throughout the world.

The same doxological note sounds again in Romans 15. Paul speaks of "the grace given me by God to be a minister of Christ Jesus to the Gentiles in the priestly service of the gospel of God, so that the offering of the Gentiles may be acceptable, sanctified by the Holy Spirit" (vv. 15–16). Paul sees preaching as a priestly service and his priestly offering as lives that are changed by the gospel message. For Paul, the work of preaching the good news is an act of devotion. It is itself worship.

And preaching is worship not for pragmatic reasons only—because we think it communicates most effectively to us some sense of God's presence and power (though it does). Preaching is worship because God is exalted in the proclamation of his grace in the midst of the assembly of his people and to the ends of the earth. It is worship *for the preacher*, whose heart and mind are engaged in an act of "expository exultation"[4] as he proclaims the truth. Preachers are fulfilling their calling as they preach. They are doing what the Lord has appointed and gifted them to do. But preaching is worship *for the hearer* too, who is but one party in a sacred exchange—a holy "conversation" in which God speaks and his people respond in praise and prayer, renewing their covenant commitments and going forth into the world to serve him. Worship, you see, is dialogical, and the preaching of the Word is "God's side" of the conversation.

Preaching and Evangelism

When we think about preaching and worship, we wonder how the two are related. Is preaching *part* of worship, or is preaching coordinate with but still distinct *from* worship? That is the struggle of most contemporary evangelicals. But what we've seen is that preaching is itself worship.

When it comes to the question of how preaching and *evangelism* relate, however, I daresay the issue has rarely even occurred to us. Evangelism, for most evangelical Christians, happens exclusively elsewhere—out among friends and family, at the workplace, on the street, on campus, or maybe on a mission trip—but evangelism, we assume, is not what the pulpit is for.

And let's be clear: personal evangelism *is* the task of every Christian, and nothing I'm saying here should be understood as undermining that. But I do want to situate personal evangelism properly. The Reformed church has a vital place for personal piety and personal devotion and personal evangelism. But it is not the *first* place. The first place is reserved for the gathered assembly of the local church on the Lord's Day. The center of the Christian life, and the engine of Christian witness, is public worship and especially the preaching of the Word of God.

The Westminster Larger Catechism tells us that "the Spirit of God makes the reading, but especially the preaching of the word, an effectual means of enlightening, convincing, and humbling sinners; of driving them out of themselves, and drawing them unto Christ; of conforming them to his image, and subduing them to his will; of strengthening them against temptations and corruptions; of building them up in grace, and establishing their hearts in holiness and comfort through faith unto salvation."[5] We should expect the Spirit of God to wield his Word in human hearts not only to produce sanctification (conforming us to Christ's image, subduing us to his will, strengthening us against temptations and corruptions, building us up in grace, and establishing our hearts in holiness and comfort through faith) but conversion too. God, we confess, has ordained "the reading, but especially the preaching of the word" to bring sinners to saving faith in Jesus. A Reformed view of evangelism starts in the pulpit.

We needn't survey many examples of New Testament preaching to demonstrate the normativity of evangelistic preaching in the Bible. Almost *all* the examples of New Testament sermons are evangelistic in nature. Whether one considers the old covenant prophetic ministry of

John the Baptist, or the preaching of Christ in the Gospels, or the ministry of Peter or Stephen or Paul in the book of Acts, we find it is done with a view to bringing people to repentance and saving faith. In 2 Timothy 4, Paul tells his young protégé, Timothy, whom he has appointed to pastor the church in Ephesus, that he must "preach the word" (v. 2). In this context, Paul then goes on to add that he must "always be sober-minded, endure suffering, do the work of an evangelist, fulfill your ministry" (v. 5). The work of an evangelist, necessary for Timothy to fulfil his ministry, is, at least in significant measure, the work of preaching.

And this was Paul's own ministry pattern. Paul declares, "Christ did not send me to baptize but to preach the gospel, and not with words of eloquent wisdom, lest the cross of Christ be emptied of its power" (1 Cor. 1:17). In other words, while other duties fall to Christian ministers, Paul was single-minded in his focus to proclaim the cross of Christ as plainly and forthrightly as he could. New Testament preaching is gospel preaching, preaching burdened with the message of the cross, preaching that presses the claims of Christ upon the consciences of all who hear and implores them, as Paul put it, to "be reconciled to God" (2 Cor. 5:20).

It is sometimes argued that preaching on Sundays is for Christians and therefore evangelistic preaching makes no sense in that context. Non-Christians aren't in church, for the most part, so they won't hear the gospel message.

And Christians who *are* present want more than a constant reminder of the call to repent and believe in Jesus.

Let me deal with the second part of that objection first. To be sure, a formulaic gospel presentation that reduces application to a simplistic call to repent and believe would become tiresome and would undoubtedly fail to nourish growing Christians. But when Paul told the Corinthians that in his preaching he resolved to know nothing among them "except Jesus Christ and him crucified" (1 Cor. 2:2), he did not mean that he would preach the same message over and over each week. Rather, Paul would deal with all sorts of practical and pressing concerns facing the church in light of who Jesus is and what he came to do. He brought the good news about "Christ and him crucified" to bear upon every theological and ethical challenge and demonstrated how the gospel is the deep well from which believers must always and continually draw their nourishment and satisfaction.

This is actually the pattern reflected in the letter of 1 Corinthians itself, shaped as it is by the various needs confronting the Corinthian church. A glance at the letter will demonstrate that at each point of his argument Paul brought Christ and the gospel message to bear upon the specific issue at hand. The letter itself embodies the principle that informed Paul's ministry while he was with them and reminds us that gospel preaching remains profoundly practical for the lives of believers as well as for the unconverted.

Moreover, when Christians do hear robust evangelistic calls directed at the unconverted, it ought not to frustrate or disappoint them, as if this message had no bearing upon them. Instead, it ought to inflame their hearts and thrill their souls. They ought to find themselves fighting the urge to turn around in their chairs to see who has been gripped by the call of God in the gospel. They ought to rejoice in the glorious message that has saved them and find their hearts burning afresh with zeal that God might work in others through this message as he has in them. Good evangelistic preaching should thrill believers, never bore them.

And that brings us to the first part of the objection. "Surely," the objector wonders, "evangelistic preaching from the pulpit misses the mark. After all, evangelism isn't for the church but for the world. The pulpit is the wrong place for it." Not so! Thom Rainer surveyed formerly unchurched people who came to faith in Christ about the most compelling factors that drew them to become committed members of a local church. His findings challenge the assumption that preaching is an evangelistically ineffective strategy: "We are hearing from the formerly unchurched that preaching that truly teaches the Bible in its original context is a major factor in reaching the unchurched. Indeed, this issue was mentioned by 211 of our 353 survey respondents. The formerly unchurched told us that they were attracted to strong biblical teaching and to understanding Christian doctrine. Pastors who understand this and who communicate doctrine clearly are among the leaders whose churches are reaching the unchurched."[6]

In fact, when the pulpit is consistently evangelistic and full of the gospel, there are a number of important practical benefits for the life of the congregation as a whole and for the welfare of those who respond to the message. First, as Mark Dever has pointed out, "What you win them *with* is likely what you'll win them *to*. If you win them with the Gospel, you'll win them to the Gospel. If you win them with technique, programs, entertainment, and personal charisma, you might end up winning them to yourself and your methods (and you might not!), but it's likely that they won't be won to the Gospel first and foremost."[7]

If preaching has been the principle means by which people come to Christ, it will not be difficult to introduce them to preaching as the principle means by which we expect them to grow and mature in Christ. But if we have "won" people through extraordinary events and spectacular shows, by strategies of our own invention and clever techniques we have devised, coming to church and sitting under the steady and straightforward exposition of the Bible every week will likely seem to many rather anticlimactic.

We need to be careful that we do not think ourselves smarter than God. He has ordained *preaching* for our conversion and our growth. When we opt instead for some evangelistic method of our own creation, we ought not to be surprised to find that non-Christians who are initially attracted to the church by our innovative outreach methods will not be nearly so easy to keep in the church by the regular ministry of the Word.

Moreover, when the gospel rings from the pulpit every week, and evangelistic appeals to come to Christ with urgency and pathos are not uncommon in our churches, the members of the local church can be confident in inviting their non-Christian friends along on any given Sunday, safe in the knowledge that they will always hear saving truth proclaimed. A healthy Reformed church, where the gospel has thoroughly penetrated not only the preaching but also the hearts of the hearers, will be a church whose members regularly invite their friends to come and hear the good news.

Preaching and Discipleship

Finally, we need to consider the relationship between preaching and discipleship. For many Christians, discipleship simply means "one-on-one mentoring." To make a disciple is to model Christian godliness and to train intensively a new believer toward maturity through Bible study and personal example. Rarely does expositional preaching feature in our vision of a productive discipleship program. And even when it does, it is not usually regarded as the one vital ingredient in our plan for the maturation of healthy Christians. Small-group ministries, mentoring programs, training in the latest Christian literature, podcasts, and online conference messages all receive attention, but the regular preaching of the Word of God by our own pastor, in our own congregation, week in and week out, is all too often discounted and overlooked. But Reformed churches believe that God's primary strategy for our growth as disciples lies precisely there: in the work of our own pastor every Lord's Day, shepherding us through the Word, nourishing us in the truth, and guarding us from error. Faithful preaching, we might say, is God's discipleship program, and it is focused on three things: *pastoring, providing* for, and *protecting* the flock of God.

Preaching Is Pastoring: The Preacher Must Know and Love the Sheep

Peter tells elders to "shepherd the flock of God that is among you" (1 Peter 5:2). What does shepherding involve? In Ephesians 4:11, Paul says that God "gave the apostles, the prophets, the evangelists, the shepherds and teachers to equip the saints for the work of ministry." Apostles, prophets, and evangelists held extraordinary and temporary offices[8] whose function was bound up with the foundation of the church and the inspiration and faithful communication of what became the New Testament. Of the offices in Paul's list, this leaves only "shepherds [or pastors] and teachers"—referring to not two offices but one—as continuing ministries in the contemporary church.

Gospel ministers are pastor-teachers. They are shepherds. And Paul describes the task entrusted to them as the equipping of the saints "for the work of ministry, for building up the body of Christ, until we all attain to the unity of the faith and of the knowledge of the Son of God, to mature manhood, to the measure of the stature of the fullness of Christ" (Eph. 4:12–13). The ascended Christ has given to the church pastor-teachers to equip, unify, and mature the saints.

To make the same point more simply: pastor-teachers are to shepherd us by teaching the Word in order to make mature disciples. That is why elders must be "able to give instruction in sound doctrine" (Titus 1:9). It's why the only area of special giftedness listed with the various character qualifications required of elders in 1 Timothy 3 is that they be "able to teach" (v. 2). First Timothy 5:17 speaks of elders in the churches who "labor in preaching and teaching." At the heart of the charge given to pastors is the preaching of the Word of God. It's how they shepherd us.

But of course, that entails more than a commitment on their part to deep study and careful preparation for the pulpit. In order for faithful preaching to be truly pastoral, it also requires the preacher to know the sheep, to know their needs and fears and wants and sins and struggles. He must say not only what the text of Scripture says but also what the flock needs to hear. And for that, he must know what the flock most needs. If he is to be a skillful shepherd who leads his flock to green pastures and quiet waters that their souls might be restored, he must love the sheep, know the sheep, and tend the sheep. A good shepherd should "smell" like his sheep. A good pastor should often be among his people.

The preaching of the Word in a faithful Reformed church is never an exercise in *mere* exposition, much less in abstract theological discourse or rhetorical display. While the Reformed preacher's burden is certainly to be faithful to the text, that very commitment demands that he bring the text to bear on the people of God, for whose benefit God gave the text in the first place. It is a terrible indictment of the pulpit ministry in any church when a minister's hearers conclude after listening to him that he loves his books more than he loves them.

Preaching Is Providing: The Preacher Must Feed the Sheep

If preaching is basic to God's discipleship program, and he has called pastors to proclaim his Word with Christian discipleship in view, it follows that the preacher must faithfully nourish his hearers with a rich and balanced diet of biblical instruction. This is another argument in support of the systematic, consecutive exposition of whole Bible books as the primary preaching method in healthy pulpits and churches. By following this pattern,

preaching covers the whole text. It does not avoid difficult passages. It does not skirt the moral and theological
conundrums. The preacher must face them and find in
them God's purpose for the edification of his hearers, and
in so doing, he helps us to learn not just what the text
means but *how to read the text for ourselves*. God has given
all sixty-six books of Holy Scripture for our instruction
and spiritual formation. Some are harder to understand
than others. But we need exposure to them all. There
ought to be no "no-go" areas in our Bibles. It is the preacher's duty to take his people by the hand and to lead them
into the whole Bible, the harder passages no less than the
more accessible ones, and to show them how to mine the
riches that are to be found there for themselves.

Furthermore, when the pastor is really engaged with
his flock, he will know the apologetic concerns that con-
front them. He will feel the urgency of the questions his
people are asking when tragedy or natural disaster or
inexplicable suffering strikes the community. He will be
ready to speak a word from the Lord for all such occasions, showing as he does that the Bible is *always* relevant.
It never needs to be *made* relevant.

In my own ministry of simply preaching the text, I
have found that very often when tragedy penetrates the
life of the congregation, in God's wonderful providence
the next passage in line for that Sunday already has much
to say to us just when we need it most. Faithful Reformed
expository preaching does not preach over the top of the

congregation's concerns. It preaches the Word to the congregation's concerns.

The call to provide spiritual nourishment for the flock also means that biblical instruction from the pulpit must target the *needs*, not the *wants* and *tastes*, of the congregation. A predecessor of mine in a church I formerly served was once taken aside by a major donor after a sermon and told, "You just remember who paid for the new sound system, boy!" He was being warned not to step on his toes or to push particular truths too hard. But even when such obvious hostility is not present, a preacher may know that there are widespread and spiritually dangerous patterns that need to be addressed in his ministry if he is really to help his congregation. For example, affluence, and the idols of money and self-reliance and reputation and keeping up appearances that often go with it, will need to be gently but boldly addressed and lovingly confronted with biblical rebuke and gospel mercy.

But to do so is scary. The preacher risks much. People don't like to have their sins exposed. And let's be honest: as we listen to preaching, it's easy to be lazy and to prefer upbeat, short, unchallenging messages that do not require much thought. We want digestible, white-bread sermons that won't take much chewing to fill us up. "So, pastor, keep it short and sweet. Tell us more stories. Make us laugh a little. Leave us with a spring in our step and a song in our hearts!" Faithful preaching should never be dry or dull or burdensome, but the preacher's duty to God and his congregation is not to tell them what they want to hear—any more than a mother's duty to her children is to feed them M&Ms instead of a nutritious dinner because that's what they prefer. Faithful Reformed preaching will aim at theological depth. It will seek to stimulate and provoke deep thought. While it will always try to speak in such a way that a new Christian will understand, it will also provide such instruction that a mature believer will be challenged. It will not dumb down or soft-pedal the truth of God. Its goal is to help us to grow up.

Preaching Is Protecting: The Preacher Must Warn and Guard the Sheep

A third part of the discipleship role of faithful preaching has to do with protecting the flock. The apostle Paul charges the elders of the church at Ephesus in the following terms:

> Pay careful attention to yourselves and to all the flock, in which the Holy Spirit has made you overseers, to care for the church of God, which he obtained with his own blood. I know that after my departure fierce wolves will come in among you, not sparing the flock; and from among your own selves will arise men speaking twisted things, to draw away the disciples after them. Therefore be alert, remembering that for three years I did not cease night or day to admonish every one with tears. And now I commend you to God and

> to the word of his grace, which is able to build you up
> and to give you the inheritance among all those who
> are sanctified. (Acts 20:28–32)

Paul's burden is for the protection of the church from predatory false teachers. Strikingly, the attack will come from the ranks of the church's own Bible teachers, who will begin to speak "twisted things," resulting in division. To combat this, the apostle calls the elders to special vigilance, and he reminds them of his own pastoral example of faithful biblical instruction, "admonish[ing] every one with tears." That is how he wants them to respond to the problem of error when it comes.

Preaching accomplishes that objective both positively and negatively. It is said that when anti-fraud law enforcement agents are being trained to detect counterfeit bills, they spend very little time examining forgeries and the bulk of their time closely examining genuine currency, because the best defense against a fake is to know what the real thing looks like. Similarly, when it comes to false teaching, the best defense against error is the truth. The positive exposition of the Bible, the careful teaching of all the doctrines of Holy Scripture, showing their various parts and how they relate one to another, will do far more to guard the flock against false doctrine than any exposé of error ever could. This approach should be primary. Something is wrong in a preaching ministry when the messages are overly focused on other people's bad theology.

A critical spirit and a defensive posture will soon alienate the listener and marginalize the church.

Good preaching will not raise controversies that the congregation are not facing. The preacher may be anxious about theological drift in this or that area of his denomination, for example. But if his congregation remains untroubled by those trends, he must be very careful about raising them in his regular ministry. The danger is that he will raise questions no one has yet thought to ask and so awaken curiosity about the very mistakes he is trying to avoid. We are all easily fascinated by strange new ideas, and we shouldn't point them out if they have not yet begun to gain traction on their own. Faithful preaching will be content to teach the truth positively, resting in the conviction that a deep acquaintance with the truth will always be the best defense against error.

But when false teaching creeps into a church's life, the preacher must not shrink from addressing it. Paul told Timothy, "As I urged you when I was going to Macedonia, remain at Ephesus so that you may charge certain persons not to teach any different doctrine" (1 Tim. 1:3). And the apostle told Titus, "There are many who are insubordinate, empty talkers and deceivers, especially those of the circumcision party. They must be silenced, since they are upsetting whole families by teaching for shameful gain what they ought not to teach" (Titus 1:10–11). Timothy in Ephesus and Titus in Crete were both given the same charge: they must counter directly the false teaching that had penetrated the congregations in those places. It is an unpleasant but sometimes necessary part of faithful preaching to warn the congregation about counterfeit doctrine and false teachers and to expose their errors with force and vigor.

In sum, preaching in a Reformed church is much more than imparting data. It is not a performance or a pep talk or a stand-up routine. We benefit from it not simply by learning something new or by being swept along by the oratory. In preaching, something much more profound is taking place. It is the climax of worship. It is the mouth of God. When someone says, "I wish God would speak to me," Reformed Christians reply, "He has and he will . . . in the reading and preaching of the Bible." Preaching cannot be evaluated on the basis of how effective it is as a communication strategy alone. It is a transcendent event in which God himself comes to us and we hear him speak.

Because preaching is such a momentous thing, it ought not to be a surprise to discover that it is God's ordained means by which to bring people to Christ. Good preaching exposes sin and helps people to see their need of a savior. It seeks to shatter every excuse for failing to come to him, and it presses his offer of mercy and grace upon the conscience with urgency and pathos. Some churches confine evangelism to the private conversations of Christians with non-Christian friends. Others think that Sunday worship should be transformed into an event, an entertaining stage production, in the hopes that they can attract visitors to the congregation. But the Reformed tradition views the exposition of the Word of God as the way God is most often pleased to work in bringing sinners to a saving knowledge of Christ. There is no show, no attempt to ape the entertainments of the world. The clear declaration of the message of the cross is mighty to save, and faithful Reformed preaching will always seek to put it front and center.

But the work of God in preaching is not finished when a person is converted. The same word that wins us to Christ grows us in Christ. Preaching is about evangelism, but it is also about discipleship. Small-group Bible study and one-on-one mentoring relationships have an important role in helping Christians to grow up in Christ. But preaching the Bible faithfully and clearly is the principle means of discipleship and growth in Reformed churches. Such preaching pastors the flock, caring for them with understanding and tenderness. It provides for the flock a rich and nourishing spiritual diet, always taking care to provide what is needed, even if it is not always what is wanted. And faithful preaching protects the flock from wolves who seek to harm the sheep by peddling error. This is how we grow into what Paul calls "mature manhood, to the measure of the stature of the fullness of Christ, so that we may no longer be children, tossed to and fro by the waves and carried about by every wind of doctrine" (Eph. 4:13–14). In short, faithful Reformed preaching *is* worship, evangelism, and discipleship.

Questions for Further Reflection

1. Why do we sometimes forget that listening to preaching is an act of worship? How does this understanding change how we listen?

2. Is inviting unconverted friends to church a regular part of your evangelistic strategy? If not, why? If you knew that the preaching you heard at church was regularly evangelistic in message and application, would you be more likely to bring non-Christian friends on Sunday?

3. Do you expect the primary means of your own Christian growth to be the preaching of the Word? If not, what does this tell you about your view of the importance of preaching in your Christian life?

4

GETTING THE MOST OUT OF EXPOSITIONAL PREACHING

When I was a teenager, I often failed to do what my parents asked of me in a timely and adequate manner. At the root of my problem, they had often to point out, was the fact that I "just didn't listen." In many ways, a failure to listen lies at the root of most of our struggles to grow as Christians. We hear partially. We hear what pleases us and edit out the rest. We mishear. We ignore. We reinterpret what we hear. It's not simply that we have failed to understand what God is saying to us. It's that we have preferred not to listen.

Jesus's famous parable of the sower in Luke 8 outlines various responses to the Word of God. Given how famous the parable is, the passage that follows is often overlooked, yet it has much to say to us about how we listen to God in the preaching of his Word. First, Jesus imagines a ridiculous scenario: lighting a lamp and then putting it under a jar or a bed. This, of course, defeats the purpose of lighting it. It makes no sense. Instead, the lamp goes "on a stand, so that those who enter may see the light" (v. 16). That's why we light lamps. In the context of the chapter, read alongside the parable of the sower, Jesus is saying that those who have received the Word in faith are like lamps that have been lit. Their purpose is to shine the light of the Word in such a way that others might be drawn to it and welcomed in.

Jesus reinforces that point with this principle: "Nothing is hidden that will not be made manifest, nor is anything secret that will not be known and come to light" (v. 17). To understand what is being said here, we should not miss how Jesus uses the same language to talk about his own message. He tells the disciples, "To you it has been given to know the secrets of the kingdom of God" (v. 10). In other words, the message of the gospel that Jesus preached is "the secrets of the kingdom" that must be revealed. It is the light that ignites the lamp of our lives. And that light must not be hidden but must shine so that others may see it too.

Well, so what? What difference should Jesus's teaching about the Word here really make? Jesus drives home the implications: "Take care then how you hear, for to the one who has, more will be given, and from the one who has not, even what he thinks that he has will be taken away" (v. 18). This verse serves as a conclusion for the whole section of Luke 8, beginning with the parable of the sower, that deals with the way the Word of God works. Verse 18 tells us that the key issue, the vital factor, must be how we hear the Word.

Hebrews 2:1 makes a similar point. The author urges his readers to "pay much closer attention to what we have heard, lest we drift away from it." When it comes to the way we listen to preaching, the stakes are far higher than we may at first imagine. Hebrews 2:1 warns us of spiritual drift. Luke 8:18 goes even further and warns of eternal consequences if we "have not" when, through the preaching of the Word, every opportunity to "have" has been afforded us. So what does it mean to take care how we hear? How shall we "pay much closer attention to what we have heard"? These are the questions we hope to answer in this chapter. Put more directly, we need to know how we can get the most from expositional preaching.

The Westminster Larger Catechism offers some important help. It asks, "What is required of those that hear the word preached?" and answers, "It is required of those that hear the word preached, that they attend upon it with diligence, preparation, and prayer; examine what they hear by the scriptures; receive the truth with faith, love, meekness, and readiness of mind, as the word of God; meditate, and confer of it; hide it in their hearts, and bring forth the fruit of it in their lives."[1] Let's consider that answer one phrase at a time.

Before Preaching: Prepare to Hear the Word

If we are going to get the most out of the preaching that we hear, the catechism says that *before* and *as* we come to hear the Word preached, we need "diligence, preparation, and prayer." So, how should we prepare to hear preaching?

Pray for the preacher as he prepares to preach during the week. Ask the Lord to guide him in understanding the passage and in seeing how best to illustrate its message and apply its truth to the hearts of the people.

Read the passage in advance. If you know what the preacher's text will be, try to take the time to familiarize yourself with it. Perhaps in your daily devotions read it over prayerfully and ask key questions of it, such as (1) What in it is difficult to understand? (2) How does it fit with what precedes and follows it? (3) What is its central idea? (4) What does it say about God the Father, Son, or Spirit? (5) What about sin and grace? (6) How does it challenge or comfort or encourage you? In family worship, you might read the passage over with your children and talk to them about it, perhaps in the context of discussing and applying lessons from the sermon of the week before.

Pray for a receptive and teachable heart. Ask God to help you to receive his Word in meekness and faith. Pray for a readiness to embrace the truth of God without distortion or argument, and pray for grace to believe and obey it.

Take steps to put your house in order at least by Saturday night. It is sometimes joked that the hour before Sunday morning worship is the least sanctified in any family's life. Parents are stressed. Children aren't ready. "Where are the car keys?" "You had them last!" "No, *you* did!" "What do you mean you can only find one shoe?" "*Just get in the car!*" By the time you arrive at church, no one is speaking. It's hard to concentrate on the Word with a calm and receptive heart after that, so prepare the day before. Find *both* shoes. Locate the keys. Put gas in the car. Have a clear plan for lunch.

Bring your own Bibles to church. Some people use a Bible app on their smartphone. Some churches print the passage in their bulletin. Most churches have a pew Bible available for worshippers to use. But when you bring the Bible you regularly read in private devotions to church, you are reminding yourself that hearing the preaching of the Word is part of the core disciplines by which you cultivate your spiritual health. When the preacher announces his text and you open your own Bible to the passage, you find underlines and handwritten notes there and a card from a dear friend quoting that very passage for your encouragement from years ago. Bringing your Bible to church reinforces the personal intimacy of what is really happening in preaching. A Bible app or even a pew Bible are impersonal. Your well-thumbed Bible filled with your notes and your memories drives home the point that in preaching God is speaking to you personally and specifically. Your expectation of fellowship with God in preaching will grow when the principal tool of your fellowship with him throughout the week is the same as it is on Sunday. Bring your own Bible to church!

During Preaching: Become an Active Listener

Next, the catechism says that *during* the preaching of the Word, we should be active listeners, not passive consumers. Hearers are to "examine what they hear by the scriptures; receive the truth with faith, love, meekness, and readiness of mind, as the word of God." Here are some suggestions to help you to become an active listener as the Word is preached.

Pray! The catechism doesn't say it, but this is the right place to start. As the preacher goes to the pulpit, pray for him and for the congregation and for yourself. Ask the Holy Spirit to make the Word effective. Ask God to help you to embrace what he is teaching you. Pray for the unconverted who may be present that they might be saved through the preaching of the gospel.

Cultivate godly affections that correspond to the truth. The catechism mentions three in particular. We are to receive the word "with faith, love, meekness." If listening to preaching is a vital part of our worship, then our attitude toward the message really matters. We're not to be critical judges, assessing the message and comparing its delivery to that of our favorite celebrity preachers. We are not to be self-appointed doctrinal police, constantly scanning for error so that we can pounce with glee on the poor pastor's mistakes. Let's avoid imitating the scribes and the Pharisees who constantly tested Jesus, "lying in wait for him, to catch him in something he might say" (Luke 11:54). We are to hear the Word with godward affections.

The catechism mentions *faith* first. Hebrews 4:2 reminds us that the generation of Israelites who perished in the wilderness failed to enter the land of Canaan because "the message they heard did not benefit them, because they were not united by faith with those who listened." Faith is necessary if we are to benefit from the Word. Ask God to help you to truly believe what he has said and to trust in it today and tomorrow and in the years ahead.

Next, the catechism mentions *love*. Jesus said, "If anyone loves me, he will keep my word" (John 14:23). Love obeys the Word of God. It takes what faith believes and puts it to work. It keeps Christ's commandments (see John 14:15). It's not good enough merely to *know* the Word. We must learn to *love* it and to say with the psalmist, "I find my delight in your commandments, which I love" (Ps. 119:47).

Finally, the catechism mentions *meekness*. James 1:21 reminds us that we are to "put away all filthiness and rampant wickedness and receive with meekness the implanted word, which is able to save your souls." Meekly receiving the Word, James is telling us, is basic to dealing with the deep festering sins of our hearts. Meekness means refusing to presume that we know better than God. It is the one essential ingredient in a teachable spirit.

Remind yourself that God is talking. The catechism says we are to receive the Word "with readiness of mind, as the word of God." When the Thessalonians heard the Word preached from Paul, they "accepted it not as the word of men but as what it really is, the word of God, which is at work in you believers" (1 Thess. 2:13). On Sunday as you turn the pages in your Bible to the passage announced by the preacher, quietly confess the truth to yourself once again: "God is about to speak. The Lord is talking. I have an audience with the great King of Kings." The Lord declares, "This is the one to whom I will look: he who is humble and contrite in spirit and trembles at my word" (Isa. 66:2). If you cannot get your head and heart to feel the weight of what is happening in the preaching of the Word, you will not likely tremble under its weighty glories.

Examine what you hear. The catechism says we should "examine" the message we are listening to by comparing it to other places in Scripture. We must learn to compare Scripture with Scripture. Speaking as a preacher, it is always an encouragement to hear the rustle of Bible pages as people look up cross-references and follow supporting passages mentioned in the sermon. I know that these folks are thoroughly engaged and really want to get the most from what they hear. We must strive to be Bereans, who were "more noble than those in Thessalonica" because "they received the word with all eagerness, examining the Scriptures daily to see if these things were so" (Acts 17:11).

"Examining what we hear" should also involve asking good questions of the sermon while we're listening: What is the main point of the sermon, and is it the same as the main point of the text? Has the preacher made his case and established his argument? What are his subpoints, and do they contribute to his main point? Can you see both the main points and the subpoints from this passage? What unanswered theological or practical questions did the sermon raise for you? Were the illustrations helpful in illuminating the text or the truth proclaimed, or were they mainly there for rhetorical effect and emotional appeal? How did he apply the passage? What difference should this message make in your life, in your marriage, in your parenting, in your business dealings?

Make notes. The catechism urges "readiness of mind" as we listen to preaching. We've all come to church tired and fought valiantly against the soporific effects of the preacher's voice. I once preached an impassioned sermon about the glory of God during which I thundered boldly, "How can you sleep through the preaching of the Word when God, the Lord of glory, is talking to you?"

And then, with my hands still hanging in the air and my voice still lingering in the rafters, I looked down to see my two children—who were then about five and seven years old—lying, horizontal, on the front pew, sound asleep and snoring. Needless to say, the rhetorical impact of my question was significantly blunted for the giggling congregation. Nodding off, getting distracted, zoning out: it happens to us all. But if God is talking, we ought to take steps to avoid losing focus.

Taking notes is an excellent way to maintain concentration and "readiness of mind." Have a notebook that you keep with your Bible. Record the date and time and text and title of the sermon. Write out the main headings and subpoints. Note any illustrations, phrases, questions, or applications that you found especially helpful. Try to capture not necessarily every word but the gist of each part of the sermon. If you have cultivated the art of asking questions of the sermon, you might note them here.

After Preaching: Bear Fruit

When the sermon is concluded, the catechism urges us to "meditate, and confer of it; hide it in [our] hearts, and bring forth the fruit of it in [our] lives." Notice the wisdom of each part of this instruction.

Meditate on the truth. In your daily devotions, you might read through Bible books a little at a time, aiming to cover the whole Bible in a year or two. You might have a plan to structure your prayers so that you are adoring God, confessing sin, and interceding for others. But do you have a plan to meditate on the Word of God? Sunday's sermon can be fertile soil for such meditation. One important benefit from taking decent notes is the ability to review them later. We can go back and reread the passage and think through the various points of the sermon, seeking to draw from it all the benefit we can. Turn each main point into praise and prayer. Take one subpoint a day and examine it from all angles, turning it over in your mind, bringing other Scripture to bear that touches on the same theme. Pray through its implications. Rest in its comforts. Rejoice in its promises.

Confer with others about the message. When the catechism says we should "confer of" the sermon, it means that we should make the sermon our conversation partner and come back to it often, like a wise counselor, for help and encouragement throughout the week. But this language of conferring points us in another helpful direction too. We should "confer" not only with the sermon but also with others about the sermon. Talk about the message with your friends and family.

Now, this is not an encouragement to enjoy a fine Sunday lunch of roast preacher. Let's not sanctify our sin by pretending that we are having a "good discussion about the sermon" when we are really tearing strips off the poor man who delivered it. When I say that we should confer with others on the message, I mean that we should talk about what we learned and encourage one another in the truth.

Often sincere discussion of the message preached provides some of the sweetest seasons of Christian fellowship, as we are each enriched by the insights of others. During the sermon, you may have noted some specific questions, perhaps arising from some complexity in the passage or perhaps squaring the teaching of this text with what the Bible says elsewhere. Ask godly friends for their opinion. Email the preacher and ask for his thoughts. Done carefully, such questions are deeply encouraging for those of us who preach because they reveal a mind and a heart that is serious about the Word. We think, "Here is someone who has really listened and who wants to grow." Your questions are welcome. But you might also try taking a look at a commentary. Do some digging of your own. Confer not just with the living people of God in your church but also with the saints of previous generations, whose writings provide a treasure trove of wisdom. Who knows what other riches you might find!

Memorize what matters most. The catechism recommends that we commit to memory lessons that God has taught us. We should hide them in our hearts. If it's helpful, it's worth remembering. A quote from the sermon, an insight into a difficult passage you've always struggled with, a helpful way to apply a challenging principle to today's problems: these are all worth committing to memory for future use. If God has worked through the text in a sermon, why not spend the next week memorizing the passage? Break it down into short phrases. Say it out loud to yourself. Pray it into your memory. Quote it to others during the day. Make the memorized text like the memorial stone Samuel erected at Ebenezer, saying, "Till now the LORD has helped us" (1 Sam. 7:12). Memorizing that passage aids you to recall the ways the Lord has dealt graciously with you through the message and helps to fuel gratitude and praise in days to come.

Develop an action plan. The catechism reminds us that our supreme responsibility as we listen to the Word is to bring forth the fruit of it in our lives. We must be "doers of the Word, and not hearers only" (James 1:22). We should seek, in concrete ways, to implement what we have learned from God in the Scriptures throughout the coming week. As you review your notes and remember the specific applications made in the sermon, ask yourself, "How can I put this into practice today, tomorrow, and next week? What needs to change? Who do I need to talk to about accountability? What problem has this message uncovered that I ought to make a matter of serious, ongoing prayer?"

If we come to the preaching of the Word of God like this, not only will we benefit immensely from what we hear but also God will be glorified and his people helped and encouraged as they see us being transformed by the renewal of our minds (see Rom. 12:2).

Questions for Further Reflection

1. In what areas in your life are there barriers to your hearing the preaching of the Word? What practical steps can you take to improve in these areas?

2. How do you currently listen to preaching? Are you able to concentrate? What are the main distractions for you? How can you mitigate or overcome them?

3. Have you ever revisited your sermon notes? What about listening again to a sermon that you found helpful? How can you and your household make the most of what you've heard throughout the course of the week? Are there ways you can connect your daily devotions to the weekly preaching?

QUESTIONS AND ANSWERS ON PREACHING

Preaching faces many challenges today, and understanding why it still matters and what we can expect God to do through it remain urgent concerns. Throughout this book, I've tried to make a case for preaching that will help you to answer many questions for yourself. However, several issues still remain. In what follows, I've tried to provide short(ish!) answers to some of the most common questions. If this section doesn't quite address your concerns, there are recommended resources at the end of this book that can take you further still.

Why has God chosen preaching as the primary means of grace? It seems such an inefficient means of communication.

God has chosen preaching as the primary means of grace because God is a talking God. He spoke creation into being and "upholds the universe by the word of his power" (Heb. 1:3; see also Gen. 1). And by means of "the living and abiding word of God," we are "born again, not of perishable seed but of imperishable" (1 Peter 1:23). The way God has chosen to reveal himself to us is by his Word.

When God spoke to his people at Horeb in Deuteronomy 4, Moses pointed out that "you heard the sound of words, but saw no form; there was only a voice" (v. 12). God cannot be comprehended by the imagination of the human mind. That is why ours is a liturgy of listening. He speaks to us. We hear him. We do not see him, and we are not focused on images and outward forms but on Scripture. Preaching is the appointed means of proclaiming the message of Scripture, teaching its truth, and applying its insights that best reflects the nature of Scripture itself. It follows the text and expounds the text and drives all who hear to attend closely to the text.

Furthermore, God loves to accomplish his purposes through methods that do not line up with the wisdom of the world. We have developed all sorts of sophisticated communication technologies, and communication techniques have been the subjects of sustained academic and professional study in universities and multinational corporations for decades. We are used to efficiency, immediacy, and vibrant visual stimuli, all leveraged to convey a point in under three minutes. And then we come to church . . . and the message is a thirty-five-minute monologue explaining the meaning of a two-thousand-year-old text. The experience can be jarring, no doubt. But, as Paul reminds us in 1 Corinthians 1, "it pleased God through the folly of [preaching] to save those who believe" (v. 21).

God delights to choose

what is foolish in the world to shame the wise; God chose what is weak in the world to shame the strong; God chose what is low and despised in the world, even things that are not, to bring to nothing things that are, so that no human being might boast in the presence of God. (vv. 27–29)

Preaching is apparent folly as a method because the message of the cross, on the face of it, is foolishness (see v. 27), and the people God delights to save are not usually wise and powerful or of noble birth (see v. 26). Preaching is *cruciform*. It is as improbable and unimpressive in the world's eyes as the cross. And that is why God has chosen it, that all the glory might be his.

Preaching is all well and good, I suppose, but do we need to focus on it quite so much?

The sin of our first parents in Eden was precipitated by the devil's attempt to undermine the centrality of the Word of God: "Did God actually say . . . ?" (Gen. 3:1). The temptation to be impatient with Word-centeredness in our Christian lives, and especially with the centrality of preaching in the worship of the church, is only another example of that age-old Satanic strategy of leading us to

believe that we are wiser than God. "*Did* God actually say
. . . ? *Can* the Word really be trusted? Do we *really* need to
focus on the Bible quite so much? Surely some other way,
less demanding, easier to digest, more efficient, more
appealing, can be found to do God's work!" These are lies
from the Evil One, and we do well to beware of them.

**You said that the preaching of the Word of God is the
Word of God. Does that mean that everything my
pastor says in the pulpit is infallible?**

While we pastors might sometimes think ourselves
infallible, nothing could be further from the truth! What
is infallible is the Bible, and when the pastor faithfully
and accurately explains and applies the Bible in a manner
consistent with the Bible itself, what he says has all the
authority of God speaking in his Word.

The Reformation-era slogan that the preaching of the
Word of God is the Word of God assumes the fidelity of
the sermon to the text of the Holy Scriptures. It is not
meant to be weaponized by power-hungry pastors who
want to bind consciences and command unquestioning
obedience to their every pulpit utterance. We are not
exchanging the papal claim to infallibility for a similar
claim for our sermons. We are saying, rather, that the
authority of the Word of God not only encompasses the
specific words in which the Scriptures were inspired but
also includes the ideas (and the implications of those
ideas) conveyed by the text. The work of expositional

preaching is to open up the meaning of the words and phrases and sentences and paragraphs of the Bible in such a way that the ideas and implications communicated in the text are clearly perceived by all who hear them. Such preaching is the voice of the risen Christ to us.

What can I get from expositional preaching that I can't get in my quiet time?

First, we have access to the carefully studied and prepared meditations of a trained pastor who has spent many hours poring over the text of Scripture and consulting the best insights of past and present scholarship. Simply by virtue of the time and the training afforded to your pastor, you will get much more from the same passage in his sermon than you are likely to get from a relatively brief period of private meditation at home.

Second, since our quiet times are necessarily private and individual, we tend to focus on applying the Scriptures to our individual needs. But in the public preaching of the Word, we are helped to see how the Bible speaks not only to one's own limited horizons but also to a range of issues we might never have considered. In public preaching, we are challenged and disciplined in ways we might avoid when left alone.

And third, in public preaching, surrounded as we are by our brothers and sisters in Christ, we have the opportunity to see and hear the Word of God at work in our midst. Sometimes a text that, when read privately, may have little force, grips our hearts in new ways when read and expounded in public simply because we observe that text solemnize, or comfort, or rebuke, or thrill the hearts of the people around us. Soon the mood in the room changes—a sacred stillness, or a holy wonder, or a thrill of electricity steals across the assembly as God begins to work. God's work in a neighbor's heart through the preaching of the Word is often how God underscores the importance of that same message for us.

What can I get from preaching that I can't get from my small group?

Often small groups focus on deepening the bonds of Christian fellowship. This is good and ought not to be neglected. Sometimes, however, this takes priority over the careful interpretation and application of Scripture to the hearts of the members of the group. Instead of the Bible exercising authority to discipline and redirect our thinking and living, the small group becomes a venue for the mutual exchange of opinions: "What do you think about the passage, John?" "Well I think it means X." "Huh. That's interesting. What about you, Sheila?" "Well, I like to think about it this way . . ." Some of these opinions may have something to do with the author's intention in writing the words in the text under consideration, but they typically tell us far more about the desires and interests of the person whose opinions they are than what God has to say to us. Thankfully, not all small groups are like that, and group Bible study that really wrestles with what the text says and what it means can be immensely beneficial.

But in preaching, something additional is taking place. Certainly, in faithful exposition, the goal is not to share the pastor's private opinions but instead to open up the Word to our view and to help us to see its meaning and power. But more than that, faithful preaching is *heraldic*. A preacher is not just a teacher of the Bible, helping us to understand. He is the herald of the King, proclaiming an authoritative word from the Lord. He is called to stand in the congregation and to bring the people the King's message with all its urgency and gravity and power.

The heraldic dynamic of preaching simply does not exist in a small-group Bible study. Small groups are discursive and exploratory. They are for discussion and debate and wrestling together with ideas. Healthy small groups that do that are vital. But in public preaching, we are hearing something else. To be sure, there is a didactic element. Information is being communicated. Teaching is being given. But more than that, God is talking, through his authorized spokesman, who has been called to shepherd your soul and to pastor you, by means of the Word of God.

Why do I need to come to church, since I have access to the best preaching online?

Part of God's intention for preaching is pastoral. He intends that his children be enfolded into the fellowship of particular local churches, establishing them within a web of ever-deepening relationships and under the care and oversight of loving local elders. Preaching happens in the nexus of all these elements. It presupposes relationship and pastoral bonds. It is for the welfare of your soul in the context of your own church. When we stay home and listen to our favorite preachers online instead, we are cutting ourselves off from the primary context within which preaching was always designed to be heard. What's more, in choosing online preaching over the local church, there's the danger that we will cherry-pick our favorite sermons and preachers, so that instead of what we *need*, we will only ever hear what we *like*. To do so is to have effectively privatized Christianity. It would be the triumph of the consumer culture, which argues, "If I can find a more convenient delivery system to supply what I want or need, that should always be preferred."

David Clarkson (1622–1686) was a friend and assistant minister to the great Puritan theologian John Owen. He preached an important sermon, based on Psalm 87:2—"The LORD loves the gates of Zion more than all the dwelling places of Jacob"—titled "Public Worship to Be Preferred before Private."[1] In it he observes that the phrase "the gates of Zion" points to a public venue, whereas "the dwelling places of Jacob" are the private residences of individual Hebrews. Why does the Lord love the public space more than the private one? Clarkson argues that the worship of God is public in the gates of Zion, while it's private in the dwellings of Jacob:

> But it may be replied, the Lord had worship, not only in the gates of Zion, in the temple, but also in the dwellings of Jacob. . . . Since, therefore, the worship of God was to be found in both, how can this worship be the reason why one should be preferred before the other? Surely upon no other account but this, the worship of God in the gates of Zion was public, his worship in the dwellings of Jacob was private. . . . He loved all the dwellings of Jacob, wherein he was worshipped privately; but the gates of Zion he loved more than all the dwellings of Jacob, for there he was publicly worshipped.[2]

His point is not that we must choose public *over* private worship, but rather that we must place the public worship of the church at the center of our Christian lives and view our private devotions—our "quiet times" or small groups or use of online resources like sermons and conference addresses—in a supporting role. Clarkson asks, "Is not the Lord present with his servants when they worship him in private?" In a beautiful passage, he answers, "The Lord has engaged to be with every particular saint, but when the particulars are joined in public worship, there are all the engagements united together. The Lord engages himself to let forth as it were, a stream of his comfortable, quickening presence to every particular person that fears him, but when many of these particulars join together to worship God, then these several streams are united and meet in one. So that the presence of God, which, enjoyed in private, is but a stream, in public becomes a river, a river that makes glad the city of God."[3]

There is no substitute for public ordinances, especially the public reading and preaching of the Bible. Not even the greatest online preacher of the age can pastor your soul. Only your local pastor can do that. He is the one God has appointed to care for you. His preaching, all its weaknesses notwithstanding, is the primary place where God has promised to meet you and nourish you. No online resource, however brilliant and helpful, can ever replace it.

Won't we miss out on practical topics if we commit to a church that focuses on expositional preaching? Isn't expositional preaching impractical?

To be sure, it is possible for preachers to *claim* to be engaged in expositional preaching when all they are really doing is offering a rather dry running commentary on each clause in the text. But this is not at all what we mean by expositional preaching. Faithful exposition aims to bring out what is in the text *and* to apply its truths to the hearts and lives of those who hear it, since the text itself is intended not only to *tell* us things but also to *do* things to us and in us. The Bible is both communicative and performative. And so a preacher has not been faithful to the truth he preaches if it remains abstract and unapplied and impractical. The Word of God is for life, not just for ideas.

Good exposition sticks to the Bible closely and typically works through large portions of the biblical text in a systematic way so that over several years of sitting under a faithful ministry, a congregation might hear most of the Bible preached. Given that model, unless we wish to argue that the Word of God itself is impractical, this approach will, of necessity, bring out the full array of practical and pastoral and spiritual needs that describe the human condition addressed in the Bible. Good exposition takes all its cues from Scripture. Since the Scriptures are inherently practical, this is the best way to bring the truth to bear on the varied needs of the soul.

Sometimes we need to hear more about a particular subject than a brief mention from time to time in the regular course of systematic exposition. Is there a place for topical sermons?

Absolutely! The local church or community may be facing a particular crisis, or the pastor may become aware of widespread theological misunderstandings in the congregation. These present ideal opportunities for short, topical sermon series. The preacher might helpfully trace the doctrine of God, for example, by highlighting the divine names in Scripture. Or he might take one of the seven sayings of Christ from the cross to help to unpack the character and meaning of the atonement in more detail. Sometimes a short series dealing with suffering, or with marriage, or with prayer provides timely instruction to the people of God. And when the pastor pauses a longer systematic expository series working through a Bible book to tackle these sorts of themes, he shows his flock that he is paying attention to their needs and not simply plowing on with his planned series in Deuteronomy without regard to the hurts or crises or confusions that plague the people.

But even in this scenario, the individual messages ought still to be expository in form and approach. After all, how else can we avoid merely *using* the text in service of our felt needs? No matter the subject, no matter the practical issue—parenting, marriage, guidance—the Bible has truth to bring to bear. Better to let the text speak to the issues than to let the issues determine which texts we will hear. There is no reason that a sermon series on Christian parenting, for example, couldn't be expository, and many reasons that it should be.

Why is preaching a monologue?

It has been popular among moderns to disparage monologues as fundamentally ineffective tools for communication. "We need video and PowerPoint and music and drama. Keep the monologue to a minimum. No one can pay attention for more than ten minutes to a monologue." And then along came the wildly popular TED Talks. It's not that TED Talks changed the paradigm so much as they exposed the silliness of the objection to monologues as a tool for communication. We still expect candidates for high political office to give sober and extended speeches outlining their visions for the welfare of the electorate. We still expect college classrooms to feature sometimes double periods of direct instruction, typically in lecture form. But ask people to sit for thirty minutes to listen to the exposition of the Bible and suddenly howls of protest erupt: "This is such an out-of-date communication model. You are asking too much of people. No one can possibly pay attention to this." Certainly, dull and lifeless preaching is hard to endure. I have no desire to defend bad preaching. But good preaching is dynamic, thoughtful, and engaging. It changes pace, uses story and illustrative material, makes us laugh and cry, amazes and humbles us—and does so by bringing us into the presence of God and pressing upon our consciences the claims of Jesus Christ. Nothing could be more riveting.

But there is another sense in which the claim that preaching is a monologue needs to be carefully qualified. Good preaching is never one-sided. It is always dialogical. Often, if a man is much of a pastor to his people, a glance across the congregation as he climbs into the pulpit on Sunday will identify to him the mourning and the troubled, the growing and the backsliding, the worldly and the spiritually seeking. As he begins to preach and gauges reactions, emphases that seemed to him during his preparation to be bold and challenging are now revealed as inappropriately direct and insensitive. He will adjust his tone and his language. He will speak *to* the people for their sakes and not just *at* the people with all the things he has decided they need to hear. Because all faithful preaching is an act of pastoral care, because it is the work of a shepherd who loves his flock and knows them intimately, it is never a dull lecture. It is a relational act.

It is also important to remember that preaching is the declaration of God's authoritative Word. That note of authority shouldn't be missed. If, as we've argued, God himself is talking in the faithful preaching of his Word, then there is something fundamentally immodest and presumptuous about the insistence that we have our say. We may not like the idea that we are being talked *to*. We may prefer to be talked *with*. We have much to say that is valid and helpful, after all. But while there may be a place for that—small groups once again come to mind—preaching is the one place (it may even be the only place left for some of us) where we shut up and listen to Someone address us authoritatively with urgent and vital news upon which our spiritual lives depend. In this way, preaching as an authoritative monologue teaches the important Christian virtue of humility.

Finally, if we experience (even great) preaching as a dull monologue, we ought to be willing to ask ourselves whether the problem lies not first with an allegedly outmoded communication strategy but with our own hearts. Have we come prepared to hear the Word of the Lord? Have we broken up the stony ground of our hearts in prayer before coming? Do we take notes? Do we pray while the pastor preaches, asking for ears to hear what the Holy Spirit might be saying to us? Perhaps our impatience with pulpit "monologues" is really an expression of our failure to be active listeners who engage with the Scriptures before God in the preaching of the Word.

Why do I need preaching? I have the Eucharist.

We often feel the emotional impact of the sacraments far more immediately than we do the preaching of the Word. The sensory appeal, the beauty of the ceremony, the vivid symbolism all have a profound effect upon us. A single speaker expounding the Bible, sometimes with less than comfortable things to say to us, may not appear to have much going for it by comparison. Given all that, why not simply dispense with preaching and move directly to the far more impactful celebration of the Eucharist? Or, if we *must* have preaching, then at least get it over with as quickly as humanly possible!

But there is a basic, though not uncommon, misunderstanding behind all this. We need to realize that the sacraments of baptism and the Lord's Supper cannot exist apart from the Word of God. If we were to strip the sacraments of their context in the preaching of the Word, we would no longer be celebrating sacraments at all but rather indulging our senses in a scripturally and theologically unfounded act of pure sentimentality. *The Second Book of Discipline* (1578) articulated principles of biblical church government for the fledgling Reformed church in Scotland. Donald MacLeod notes the *Second Book*'s statement that "with doctrine is joined the administration of the Sacraments" and makes the following observations:

This is not only a declaration that it is part of the duty of the minister of the Word to administer the Sacraments[4]; it is also an acknowledgement that there can be no sacrament apart from the preaching of the Word. This was in line with Augustine's oft-quoted remark, "The word is added to the element, and there results the Sacrament," but it was also something that Calvin had stressed repeatedly. . . . Calvin even went so far as to declare that the Sacraments take their virtue from the Word and that if not accompanied by preaching the "chief substance" of the Supper was lacking. It was not a question of the Word *and* Sacrament. The Word is integral to the Sacrament because without it there can be no remembrance and no thanksgiving.[5]

The misunderstanding in the question "Why do I need preaching since I have the Eucharist?" lies in the notion that there is any such thing as a sacrament without preaching. The Eucharist is an adjunct and an assistant to the gospel preached. It can never be a substitute for it. Moreover, we fail to grasp the nature of the grace communicated to us in the Lord's Supper when we think that something else is given to our faith at Communion than is given in the ministry of the Word. The fact is, however, that in the Word as in the sacraments, the grace communicated to us is the same: in both, God gives Christ to his people for our spiritual nourishment and comfort. You do not get a different Christ in the Lord's Supper than you get in preaching. In fact, it would be quite appropriate to say that the sacraments are visible words. The water of baptism and the bread and wine of Communion are forms of the Word, not something distinct from it with an existence and meaning separable from the Word. Without the Word to give them meaning and content, they remain only water, bread, and wine.

We do need the Eucharist. But we need it to be the Eucharist in all its full beauty and power, which requires that we receive it in the context of the ministry of the Word. And the need we have for the Eucharist is the same need we have for the Word itself, since the sacraments are only visible words, appended to the Word preached, to reinforce and drive home its message.

Isn't expositional preaching too intellectual?

There are three things to say in answer to this. The first would be to admit that expositional preaching does indeed appeal to the mind and requires attention and thought to truly benefit from it. That's not to say that good exposition is dry or academic or above the heads of those who listen. The best expository preaching engages the affections and motivates the will as well as instructs the intellect. Moreover, I'd argue that it does so more forcefully and fruitfully than other methods because it demonstrates the connection between the affections of the heart and the truth being expounded. We are led to feel deeply by the impact of biblical truth faithfully expounded, winsomely illustrated, and lovingly applied. But we remain persuaded that the engagement of the mind and the use of our intellect are the primary targets at which good preaching ought to take careful aim. We are to be transformed by the renewal of our minds (see Rom. 12:2). In the book of Acts, one of Luke's favorite words to describe the preaching of the apostles was "reasoning" (Acts 17:2, 17; 18:4, 19; 19:8–9; 24:25). For example, in Acts 17:2–4, we read,

> And Paul went in, as was his custom, and on three Sabbath days he reasoned with them from the Scriptures, explaining and proving that it was necessary for the Christ to suffer and to rise from the dead, and saying, "This Jesus, whom I proclaim to you, is the Christ." And some of them were persuaded and joined Paul and Silas, as did a great many of the devout Greeks and not a few of the leading women.

Paul reasoned from the Scriptures, explaining and proving, and some were persuaded. It is not possible to understand these terms without recognizing in them an appeal to the mind. Expositional preaching is "reasoning from the Scriptures, explaining and proving" with a view to persuasion.

Of course, another part of the answer has to acknowledge that bad exposition, like bad preaching, or bad music, or bad cuisine, is just bad. But let's also admit that boring, dry, intellectual preaching is not a function of the expository method per se. It is a function, rather, of the weaknesses and failures of the preacher. Paul was an expositor, after all, but, if the riots that regularly followed in the wake of his messages are any indication, he was never dull or cerebral or academic. An intellectually rigorous but stupefyingly dull sermon may be doctrinally and exegetically accurate, but it has failed, at a fundamental level, to serve the text of the Holy Scriptures. Bare intellectualism in preaching makes the Word of God look dull when it should unleash the Bible in all its electrifying power. That is why I don't hesitate to say that boring preaching is sinful. Arid intellectualism is wicked. And any preacher who does not strive to rivet the minds and affections and imaginations and wills of his hearers with the gravity and wonder of the divine message is being disobedient to God's call.

Having said that, one further point needs to be faced. It's a possibility that our struggle with expositional preaching isn't really a result of some flaw in the expository method, nor even with the weaknesses of the expositor, so much as it has to do with the steady diet of vapid sermonettes we have been content to consume for far too long. Perhaps our experience has trained us to think of preaching merely as something like a species of motivational talk: it should be light, filled with stories, always upbeat, and easily digestible without a second's thought. And, to be sure, expositional preaching will not fill that

bill. But I can't help wondering if our fears that expositional preaching is too intellectual may actually unmask
the erosion of our ability to think deeply in sustained ways
about important truths. We know that the screens and
sound bites that assail us with flashes of information at
blistering speeds have a deleterious effect on our ability to
engage with arguments and reason carefully. Our patience
with complexity and profundity has been undermined.

I do not think the solution is for the preacher to give
in, and go with the flow, and adapt his method to these
new forms of information dissemination. I think we
should recognize instead that in expositional preaching
God has provided a much-needed counter to the sound
bite and the internet meme. He has given us a long-form,
deep-dive method that takes us down into the details and
beauties of his Word in such a way that the benefit to us
lies not only in the content communicated but also in the
retraining of our minds to engage in a new and more serious way with the things that matter most.

Evangelistic preaching can't be expositional, can it?

There are some assumptions behind this question
that are worth examining. First, there is the lurking fear
that non-Christians won't be able to handle the exposition of biblical texts. And, second, there is the idea that
exposition is inimical to evangelism. It is a method ill-
suited to presenting the claims of Christ or calling sinners
to faith in him. But I take issue with these assumptions.

The idea that non-Christians can't handle exposition implies a kind of pragmatic approach that wants to find out what will "work" and that doubts that the Bible will. Exposition serves the text by pushing it to the fore and asking every hearer to engage personally and directly with its teaching. To worry that expositional preaching won't work with non-Christians is another way to say that putting the Bible front and center in evangelism is a bad idea. But do we really want to argue that the Bible isn't sufficient for the salvation of sinners? That was certainly not the view of the apostle Paul, who told Timothy,

> But as for you, continue in what you have learned and have firmly believed, knowing from whom you learned it and how from childhood you have been acquainted with the sacred writings, which are able to make you wise for salvation through faith in Christ Jesus. (2 Tim. 3:14–15)

The Scriptures were able to make Timothy "wise for salvation through faith in Christ." They are sufficient for the salvation of sinners. If, as we have argued in this book, faithful Reformed exposition will always preach Christ and his gospel in every sermon, then there is a sense in which every expositional sermon will be evangelistic. Furthermore, preachers should never assume that everyone in the congregation is truly converted. They ought to take every opportunity afforded by the text of Scripture in the regular course of preaching to call people to repentance and faith in Christ, speaking to those who may be present but who do not yet know Jesus. And then there may be times when we know that many non-Christians will be present in church. At Christmastime, for example, the church might have a special focus on evangelism in the community, recognizing that people are more inclined to attend church at that time. And so the preacher may resolve to preach from passages that placard the person and work of Christ most clearly and to apply the message especially to the consciences of the non-Christians present, calling them to come to Christ. These messages, no less than any others, should be expositional, but they will be robustly evangelistic too. Not only can expositional preaching be evangelistic, it ought to be.

Won't my children miss out, since preaching like this is often over their heads?

We are all anxious that our children love church and feel at home there. While some churches cater to young children by excusing them from public worship for some form of "children's church," in my view that's not the best approach. When we routinely exclude our children from public worship, we signal to them that the basic elements of praise and prayer and preaching are not really for them. Ironically, driven by a desire to accommodate them, we inadvertently suggest that they are not really welcome in the service.

Instead, children should be present whenever possible in the worship of the church, and though they may not understand everything the preacher says, they will take in much more than we often realize. Furthermore, when they see their parents gripped by the Word, humbled before God, changed in their behaviors at home because of something they heard on Sunday, they learn lessons about preaching and the Bible and the worship of God that are far more impactful than almost anything we could teach in children's church.

Encourage your children to bring their own Bibles to church. During the service, help them to read the Bible passage as the pastor reads his text. Help them to make some notes. Some parents ask their children to listen out for keywords in the sermon and to note how many times the pastor says words such as *Jesus*, *sin*, or *love*. Some congregations provide simple worksheets related to the sermon for young children to color and to fill in blanks. Afterward, over lunch, talk with your children about the service. Ask them what they remembered. Help them to connect the message to their own lives.

If we train our children from the beginning to sit in the service, and to participate in worship, and to listen to the sermon, we will be helping them to grow as Christians, making use of the means of grace as we expose them to the way God has ordained that disciples should be made (see Matt. 28:18–20). Certainly, they may squirm. Sometimes we will need to take them out of the service for a time. But persevere. It's worth it. Let them see you loving the ministry of the Word. They will learn to love it too.

Why should I keep sitting under expositional preaching when my squirming kids are such a distraction?

This is a related question, but it focuses less on the children and their ability to grasp what is being said in preaching and more on the parents who are frustrated and distracted and find their own ability to concentrate undermined. Why persevere with expositional preaching when your young children won't allow you to pay attention? There is no doubt that constantly squirming little ones can be distracting, and we worry that they're distracting others too, and so we barely take in what is being said because we are constantly policing our household. But let's remember that perseverance pays off and that children grow and learn to be quiet and respectful eventually. And if, as I suggest above, you engage with them about what they hear and reward them when they do, over time they will settle down. It *will* get easier! What's more, God honors faithfulness, and when you persist in bringing your children and training them to participate in church, while you may well miss parts of the sermon along the way, in the end you will know the Lord's blessing.

Another thing that may help is to remember evening worship. Of course, not every church has an evening service, but if yours does and your children are too young to attend, perhaps you and your spouse could take turns staying home so the other can go to worship. Often weary parents find respite and refreshment in such an arrangement, not to mention the freedom to hear the preached Word without keeping an eye on the children.

If your children are now older and squirming distractions are no longer a problem, perhaps you could offer to help a family that is struggling. A word of encouragement to the children, inviting one of them to sit with your children, a candy to celebrate a child who sat through church well, a note to tell the weary parents how encouraged you are by their resolve to bring their children to worship—all these make a difference and help to reinforce the point that our children are part of the church and that we are all one family in Christ. When a child is baptized in a Presbyterian church, the whole congregation takes a vow to assist the parents in the Christian nurture of their children. Here is a practical way to do just that.

What if my pastor doesn't do expository preaching?

The first thing you must be clear about is whether the gospel is being preached in your church at all. The expository method is not, in itself, an infallible guardian of orthodoxy, and the use of another approach is not necessarily an indication of doctrinal compromise. The model of preaching at your church may not be expository, and thus, from my perspective at least, may not be nearly as effective. But that is a secondary concern. Of first importance is to make certain that the good news about Jesus is accurately and faithfully proclaimed on a regular basis. "Is the pulpit orthodox?" must be your highest priority in assessing the preaching ministry of any church. If it is not, you should leave that congregation and find a church where the truth of God is taught accurately. All other things being equal, if the message of the pulpit is faithful to historic evangelical convictions, even if it is not an expositional ministry, then you can stay in good conscience.

The next thing to be sure about is whether your pastor is actually doing exposition, though not in the manner you prefer. We need to take care not to confuse a certain style of preaching with the expository method itself. Exposition, remember, is the opening up of the meaning of a specific text or texts of Scripture. Your pastor may not engage in systematic sequential exposition through whole books of the Bible. In my judgment, this method best serves the needs of the flock. But if he is careful to explain what the passage of Scripture teaches each week and to apply it to your heart as a faithful shepherd caring for his flock, you ought to be slow to complain.

But what if, after these qualifications are carefully weighed, you find that exposition is not what you hear from your pulpit? The temptation might be to say nothing, or worse, to complain to other church members, allowing frustration to mount and spread. This is neither godly nor wise. Another temptation might be to assume that you know what your pastor ought to be doing and to lecture him on how to do his job. This approach may be gripped by zeal for expository preaching and a love for the pastor and the congregation, but it lacks wisdom.

The best approach is probably to do nothing direct at first but to commit the matter to God in prayer. Pray specifically for your pastor and his preaching, making sure to express your gratitude for him (after all, it's hard to grumble when you cultivate thankfulness!). Then pray for an opportunity to speak with him about your concerns and for the wisdom to approach the issue well. After a few weeks of committing the matter to God, arrange to meet with him. I find it best to be direct and plain. Be careful not to express your concerns as complaints or criticisms. Pastors get lots of both, and they can be deeply discouraging. Instead, begin with a word of reassurance—you love him and the congregation and want this to be an encouraging conversation. Next, state your own convictions about expository preaching in a positive way, taking care to clarify what *you* mean when you use that term. Then ask questions. "What do you think about that, pastor?" "What is your philosophy of preaching?"

If, after this conversation, your pastor is still resolved to preach in a nonexpository manner, you have a decision to make. If he preaches the gospel and is faithful to the message of the Bible, you should be very slow to break fellowship with the congregation. It might help you in this to remember that, since the Reformation, the majority of the Puritans, not to mention Spurgeon and Whitefield and many others, did not customarily engage in systematic exposition of whole Bible books. Their sermons *were* expositions of a sort but were generally single texts and often did not follow any series over many weeks. Yet these men are the heroes of evangelical faith to whom we look. God used them mightily for reformation and revival. We ought to pause and ask whether we're in danger of imagining ourselves more orthodox, more exacting, in this matter of expositional preaching than Spurgeon or Whitefield. Having said all that, if you conclude that the nonexpository method is leaving you and your household starving for spiritual truth and stunting your spiritual growth, you may indeed need to look for a congregation where systematic exposition is the norm.

How can I encourage my pastor to persevere in expository preaching?

First, engage thoroughly in the preaching that you hear. Make notes. Nod. Smile. Pore over your Bible. When he says, "Turn to John 12," turn there. And when he says, "Look at verse 7," look down at verse 7. It may not seem like much, but the preacher knows from little cues like these that his hearers are engaged and following along. This in itself is a profound encouragement.

Second, send him only positive and supportive messages on Mondays. He is typically weary and often spent emotionally on Monday. He is rarely in a good place to hear critical feedback in a healthy way on Monday. If you feel you must offer such feedback, make sure it communicates love and a desire for the prosperity and fruitfulness of his ministry. As I write this, it's a Monday. I preached on a challenging passage yesterday from 1 Chronicles. An elder just texted me and asked to talk with me about the sermon. My stomach did a little backflip. Bracing myself for impact, I called him. He was seeking to understand how the historical time line of events fit together. Instead of being discouraged, I was really encouraged. Here is a man who was paying attention and thinking deeply and wanted to understand more. And he felt free to approach me about it without embarrassment. I don't think he meant to be encouraging. He just wanted help understanding. But that desire itself made my weary heart glad.

Angry complaints rarely achieve more than wounding the man God has called to shepherd you. Critical feedback is generally better communicated face-to-face than in an email or text. But a note of thanks, an expression of gratitude, a line or two telling him how God used the message, can work wonders on a Monday when the pastor looks back at the labors of the Lord's Day with a sense of discouragement and defeat.

Third, when you see growth over time in the effectiveness of his preaching, do not always assume that the preacher has improved (though I hope he will). Remember, sometimes the fruit of a faithful expository ministry over time is seen in the growing ability of the people to hear and digest and grow because of it. It may *well* be that the preacher has gotten better. But it may *also* be that

God has been dealing with you, and you've only recently begun to hear him with new ears and a receptive heart. But whatever the cause, find ways to communicate how God is at work in you through the Word. Be specific if you can. "Thanks, pastor. I really enjoyed that message" is fine. But what if you said, "I came to church yesterday so discouraged. I was losing hope. I had begun to doubt that I'd ever grow. But then you showed me what Christ has done and how he ever lives to intercede for his people. I realized that my hope is not founded on the quality of my faith or on my own strength or sense of progress but on the perfect victory of Christ and his unfailing faithfulness to me. Pastor, that changes everything!"? That would be strong encouragement indeed. Now the pastor knows that his labor is not in vain. There is fruit from his ministry. God is at work. Now he can press on.

If the pastor is relatively new to expositional preaching, be sure to let him know how much more you gain from being taken into the Word through this model of preaching than from any other. Be sure to reinforce his resolve to expound what God has said rather than what we want to hear. Remember that sometimes change requires significant courage, demanding that the pastor depart from long-standing tradition and fly in the face of expectations. Thank him for his courage and boldness. And when you overhear others saying encouraging things about the exposition of the Bible, be sure to pass them on.

RECOMMENDED RESOURCES

Ash, Christopher. *Listen Up! A Practical Guide to Listening to Sermons.* Epson, UK: Good Book Company, 2009. [This is a very short, eminently readable, and practical booklet on how to get the most out of the sermons you hear. Ash writes with clarity, good humor, and many years of pastoral experience. In the past, I've distributed this booklet to every member of each congregation I've served.]

Chester, Tim. *Hearing God's Word.* London: Inter-Varsity Press, 2017. [Chester's accessible book is another practical guide on how to make the most of preaching. It is a book-length treatment that will benefit any reader.]

Clarkson, David. "Public Worship to Be Preferred before Private." In vol. 3 of *The Works of David Clarkson*, 187–209. Edinburgh: Banner of Truth Trust, 1988. First published 1865. [Clarkson isn't speaking here about preaching, per se, but about the importance of public worship in general. It's a classic Puritan sermon: deeply practical, theologically rich, and filled with insights into the Scriptures. Like all Puritan sermons, it multiplies divisions and subpoints and has many practical "uses" (applications). This can take a bit of getting used to for modern readers, but it is well worth it. Clarkson has a particular gift for lovely word pictures and illustrations. Every Christian should read this sermon. You can usually find it free online after a simple search.]

Packer, J. I. *God Has Spoken*. London: Hodder and Stoughton, 1979. [Although not directly about preaching, this book offers an accessible theology of Scripture. If you want to be clear about why exposition best serves the church, this is a great place to start. By teaching us about the nature of the Bible, Packer shows us why preaching that drives us into a close engagement with the text really matters.]

Pink, A. W. *Profiting from the Word*. Edinburgh: Banner of Truth Trust, 1970. First published 1921. [Pink wants us to benefit from the Bible, and his meditations on how we can do that are invaluable. This book will help your private devotions as well as your engagement with the preaching that you hear.]

NOTES

Foreword

1 David E. Garland, *1 Corinthians*, Baker Exegetical Commentary on the New Testament (Grand Rapids: Baker Academic, 2003), 674.

Chapter 1: What Is the Bible?

1 Donald MacLeod, *A Faith to Live By: Understanding Christian Doctrine* (Ross-shire, UK: Chrsitian Focus Publications, 1998), 13.

2 Westminster Confession of Faith, chapter 1.10.

3 Augustine, *Questions on the Heptateuch*, 2:73, in *The Works of Saint Augustine: A Translation for the 21st Century*, vol. 14, *Writings on the Old Testament*, ed. Boniface Ramsay, trans. Joseph T. Lienhard and Sean Doyle, 1st. ser. (Hyde Park, NY: New City Press, 2016), 125.

4 "The Scottish Confession (1560)," in *Reformed Confessions of the 16th and 17th Centuries in English Translation*, vol. 2, *1552–1566*, ed. James T. Dennison Jr. (Grand Rapids: Reformation Heritage Books, 2010), 188.

5 Iain H. Murray, *The Life of Martyn Lloyd-Jones: 1899–1981* (Edinburgh: Banner of Truth Trust, 2013), 95.

6 Murray, 96.

7 Bard Thompson, *Liturgies of the Western Church* (Philadelphia: Fortress Press, 1961), 197. For a modern critical edition, see Jonathan Gibson and Mark Earngey, *Reformation Worship: Liturgies from the Past for the Present* (Greensboro, NC: New Growth Press, 2018), 300.

8 Sinclair B. Ferguson, *From the Mouth of God: Trusting, Reading, and*

Applying the Bible (Edinburgh: Banner of Truth Trust, 2014), 47.

9 Heinrich Bullinger, "The Second Helvetic Confession," chap. 1 in *The Creeds of Christendom with a History and Critical Notes*, vol. 3, *The Evangelical Protestant Creeds, With Translations*, ed. Philip Schaff (Grand Rapids: Baker Book House, 1977), 832. Some editions include a subheading, likely original to the text of the confession, that says simply and famously, "The preaching of the Word of God is the Word of God."

Chapter 2: Why Expositional Preaching?

1 See Mark 3:14; 16:15; Luke 24:46–48; Romans 10:14–15; 1 Timothy 5:17; 2 Timothy 4:1–2; Titus 1:9.

2 William Perkins, *The Art of Prophesying* (Edinburgh: Banner of Truth Trust, 1996), 9.

3 David Helm, *Expositional Preaching: How We Speak God's Word Today* (Wheaton, IL: Crossway, 2014), 13.

4 P. T. Forsyth, *Positive Preaching and the Modern Mind* (London: Independent Press, 1907), 6.

5 Timothy Keller, *Preaching: Communicating Faith in an Age of Skepticism* (New York: Viking, 2015), 33.

6 Sinclair B. Ferguson, *Some Pastors and Teachers: Reflecting a Biblical Vision of What Every Minister Is Called to Be* (Edinburgh: Banner of Truth Trust, 2017), 652.

7 Keller, *Preaching*, 36.

8 James S. Stewart, *Heralds of God* (London: Hodder and Stoughton, 1946), 12.

9 John Stott, *I Believe in Preaching* (London: Hodder and Stoughton, 1982), 131.

10 Peter Adam, *Speaking God's Words: A Practical Theology of Preaching* (Downers Grove, IL: InterVarsity Press, 1996), 128.

11 Hughes Oliphant Old, *The Reading and Preaching of the Scriptures in the Worship of the Christian Church*, vol. 2, *The Patristic Age* (Grand Rapids: Eerdmans, 1998), 173.

12 Old, 177.

13 Old, 175.

14 T. H. L. Parker, *Calvin's Preaching* (Edinburgh: T & T Clark, 1992), 60.

15 Parker, 63.

16 Parker, 63.

17 John Gerstner, "Calvin's Two-Voice Theory of Preaching," *Reformed Reviews* 13, no. 2 (1959): 21. Quoted in Joel R. Beeke, *Reformed Preaching: Proclaiming God's Word from the Heart of the Preacher to the Heart of His People* (Wheaton, IL: Crossway, 2018), 116.

18 J. I. Packer, "Some Perspectives on Preaching," in *Preaching the Living Word: Addresses from the Evangelical Ministry Assembly*, ed. David Jackman (Ross-shire, UK: Christian Focus Publications, 1999), 34.

19 D. Martyn Lloyd-Jones, *Preaching and Preachers*, 40th anniv. ed. (Grand Rapids: Zondervan, 2011), 110.

20 D. Martyn Lloyd-Jones, notes of an unnamed address, in *Lloyd-Jones: Messenger of Grace*, by Iain H. Murray (Edinburgh: Banner of Truth Trust, 2008), 104.

21 One can hear this pattern in many of Lloyd-Jones's sermons that are available at the website for the Martyn Lloyd-Jones Trust: www.mljtrust.org.

22 "I had resolved to continue in the same privacy and obscurity, until at length William Farel detained me at Geneva, not so much by counsel and exhortation, as by a dreadful imprecation, which I felt to be as if God had from heaven laid his mighty hand upon me to arrest me." John Calvin, *Calvin's Commentaries*, vol. 4, *Commentary on the Book of Psalms*, trans. James Anderson (Grand Rapids: Baker Book House, 1996), xlii.

Chapter 3: Expositional Preaching and the Ministry of the Church

1 John Piper, *Expository Exultation: Christian Preaching as Worship* (Wheaton, IL: Crossway, 2018), 9.

2 Note the primary place of devotion to "the apostles' teaching" in the elements of worship in the assemblies of the church in Acts 2:42.

3 Sinclair B. Ferguson, "Preaching as Worship," in *Pulpit Aflame*, ed. Joel R. Beeke and Dustin W. Benge (Grand Rapids: Reformation Heritage Books, 2016), 87–89.

4 See Piper, *Expository Exultation*.

5 Westminster Larger Catechism, answer 155.

6 Thom S. Rainer, *Surprising Insights from the Unchurched and Proven Ways to Reach Them* (Grand Rapids: Zondervan, 2001), 58–59.

7 Mark Dever and Paul Alexander, *The Deliberate Church: Building Your Ministry on the Gospel* (Wheaton, IL: Crossway, 2005), 44.

8 There is some difference of opinion about the continuation of the office of evangelist, which many take to mean a person set apart by the church for an extraordinary task of evangelism. Without denying that some are unusually gifted in evangelism or that some pastors may be called to such work full-time, I prefer the opinion of Calvin, who argues that evangelists, meaning those who held a formal office in the New Testament, were "closely allied" to the apostles (think of Timothy and Titus), and thus, "of the five offices which are here enumerated, not more than the last two are intended to be perpetual." John Calvin, *Calvin's Commentaries*, vol. 21, *Commentaries on the Epistles of Paul to the Galatians and Ephesians*, ed. William Pringle (Grand Rapids: Baker Book House, 1993), 279–80.

Chapter 4: Getting the Most out of Expositional Preaching

1 Westminster Larger Catechism, question and answer 160.

Questions and Answers on Preaching

1 David Clarkson, "Public Worship to Be Preferred before Private," in *The Works of David Clarkson* (1865; repr., Edinburgh: Banner of Truth Trust, 1988), 3:187–209.

2 Clarkson, 187.

3 Clarkson, 190.

4 The reason only ordained teaching elders administer the sacraments is because they are bound together with the preaching and teaching ministry entrusted to these officers. The ministry of the sacraments is part of the ministry of the Word.

5 Donald MacLeod, *Therefore the Truth I Speak: Scottish Theology 1500–1700* (Ross-shire, UK: Christian Focus Publications, 2020), 109–10.